FINDING OUT FROM BOOKS

Andrew Fergus

HULTON EDUCATIONAL PUBLICATIONS

About Learning

Learning is mainly finding out.

Your teacher will *tell* you a lot of interesting facts and you will read about others in your school books. But suppose you need to find things out for yourself—perhaps because a subject especially appeals to you and you want to know more about it, perhaps because the class is doing topic work—how do you start?

One answer is to look at reference books. They are called this because you *refer* to them. That means you don't sit down and read them through from beginning to end. You simply track down the particular facts you want. Using such books takes a little practice, but once you know your way about them you can look up all sorts of useful information quite quickly.

Remember that often it is not so important actually knowing a fact as knowing where to find it. Remember too that sometimes facts will give you only the bare bones of a complicated subject—they are a starting point but will not give you a complete picture of the background. For that you need the help of other books and, most of all, the help of trained librarians.

About This Book

This book tells you about some of the kinds of reference book you can find in any good library. There are many more reference books, of course, besides those mentioned here. You will progress to the more unusual and specialized books without difficulty when you have had a little experience in the art of looking things up.

Contents

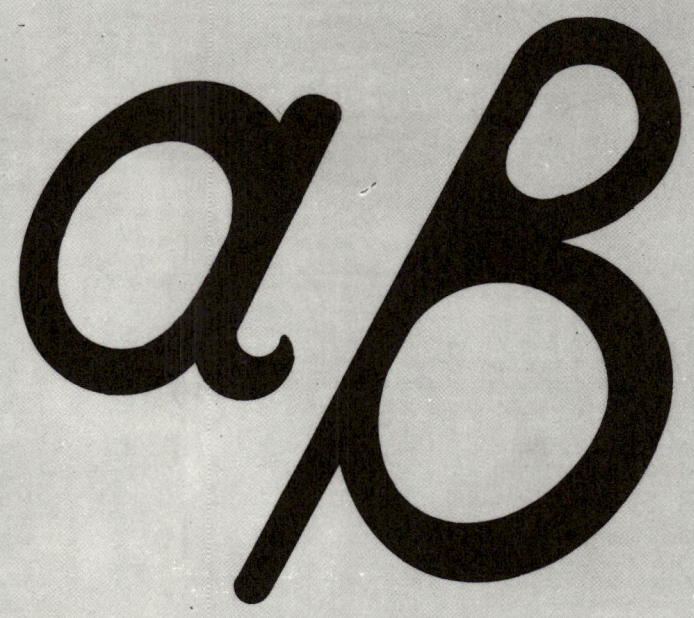

There are nearly 200 different alphabets, ancient and modern known today.

The earliest known alphabet was the Egyptian alphabet. The Egyptians used a kind of picture writing called hieroglyphics. The first letter of their alphabet was a kind of bird.

Later, for the sake of speed, they didn't draw the bird quite so carefully, but merely sketched in the rough outline.

Alphabet comes from two Greek words—alpha and beta. These were the first two letters of the Greek alphabet, so *alphabet* simply means your AB's or ABC's.

ABCDEFGHIJKLMNOPQRSTUVWXYZ

It is important to know the alphabet because reference books, such as dictionaries, are written in ABC order. ABC order (or alphabetical order) simply means that all the words beginning with A are listed first, all the words beginning with B are listed next, and so on.

Can you see a resemblance between this and any letter we use today? Can you see any resemblance to a letter in the Greek alphabet?

5

*An unusual way of learning the alphabet,
from an old ABC book.*

It is always much easier to find names if they are arranged in alphabetical order.

Name		M	T	W	Th	F	
EDWARDS J.	1	x	x	x	x	x	
HARRISON R.	2	x	x	x	O	O	
BAKER T.S.	3	x	x	x	x	x	
ISSELMAN W.	4	x	O	O	O	x	
FRAME C.	5	x	x	x	x	x	
ANDERSON A.L.	6	x	x	x	x	x	
DOUGLAS J.	7	x	x	x	x	x	
GOPEL V.	8	x	x	x	x	O	
JOHNSTONE R.	9	x	x	x	x	x	
CHARLES A.	10	x	x	x	x	x	

This is a page from a register.

Arrange the names in this register in alphabetical order.

This is known as a horn book. It was the type of book from which children were taught to read in the old days. It consisted of a little wooden bat with a piece of paper containing the alphabet pasted to it. Nailed over the paper was a piece of transparent horn to protect it and keep it clean. Children beginning to read learned the alphabet off by heart and chanted it to their teacher.

Do you think that learning the alphabet off by heart is a good way to start learning to read? Give a reason for your answer.

The rule for alphabetical order to the third letter is exactly the same.

Look at these two words.

> **untidy   unhappy**

The first two letters are the same, so we must turn to the third letter.

In *unhappy* it is H.

In *untidy* it is T.

So *unhappy* comes before *untidy*.

Alphabetical Order to the Second Letter

> **dog, axe, ebony, crow, baker, each**

It is very easy to put these words into alphabetical order—until you come to *ebony* and *each*.

They both begin with the same letter, so which one do you put first?

The rule is simple. If two words begin with the same letter, you must look at the second letter.

The second letter of *ebony* is B.
The second letter of *each* is A.

A comes before B, so *each* comes before *ebony*.

Put the following into alphabetical order:

> **effort, ewe, echo, early, Europe, editor, emerald, errand, exam, ebb, eternal, eighty, egg, elastic.**

Put the following into alphabetical order:

> **uneasy, uncle, unkind, unusual, unless, unmistakable, unwell, uniform, unable, unveil, unopened, under, unnecessary, unskilled, unpopular, unfortunate, until, unquestionably, ungainly, unhealthy, unjust, unbearable, unruly.**

Write down the surnames of all the people in your class. Arrange these surnames in an alphabetical list.

Now try it with first names.

Someone—we aren't sure who—wrote a poem in 1817 in which he cleverly used the letters of the alphabet, so that the first line had all its words beginning with A, the second had words beginning with B, and so on.

Here is the start of the poem:

An Austrian army, awfully arrayed,
Boldly by battery besieged Belgrade;
Cossack commanders cannonading come,
Dealing destruction's devastating doom.

Can you write a poem—or a sentence—something like this? Choose any subject you like.

Can you find the word that is used to describe this trick of writing? It begins with ALLIT-.

Angela's aged aunt answered Adam anxiously.

This is a sentence in which all the words begin with A.

Now see if you can complete the following sentences so that all the words in each sentence begin with the same letter:

Both boys . . . .

Cruel cannibals . . . .

Dead donkeys . . . .

Every eager Englishman . . . .

. . . . fought furiously for . . . .

Now write similar sentences for as many of the other letters of the alphabet as you can.

dĭc'tionar'ies

The first dictionaries in English were books which gave the English meanings of Latin words. They were really GLOSSARIES. Can you find out what this word means?

The first real dictionary appeared in 1721, but it was quite unlike any dictionary we know today because it did not tell the reader the *meaning* of the words. It told him the *history* of the words. Most people who could read in those days would know the meaning anyway.

The most famous early dictionary was compiled by a great writer of the 18th century—Dr. Samuel Johnson. It contained about 40,000 entries and was very long. Dr. Johnson gave no fewer than 134 meanings for the verb *take*. He spent eight years writing his dictionary.

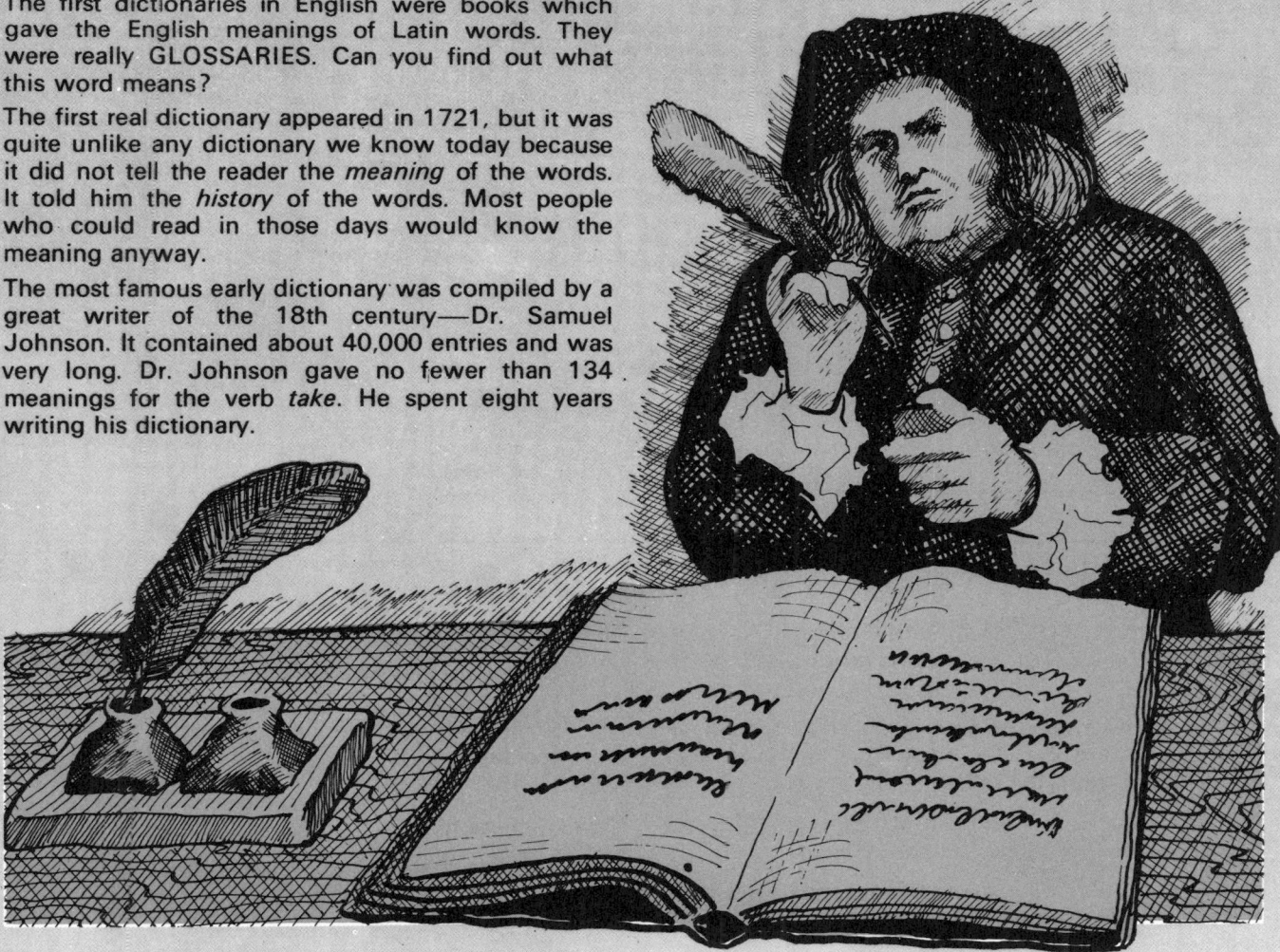

Another great name in the history of dictionaries is that of Noah Webster (1758–1843) who was born in Connecticut and educated at Yale.

He had a varied career as a journalist, lawyer and newspaper editor and first became famous for a spelling book published in 1783. Over a million copies a year were sold for use in American schools.

In 1828 he published his great work, the American Dictionary of the English Language in two volumes, with 12,000 words. In 1840 a second edition appeared and since then the dictionary has been revised several times. Noah Webster had the idea of making spelling simpler, and wrote words as they sounded. That is why Americans today write 'color' and 'labor' while English people write 'colour' and 'labour'.

How would English people spell these words?

catalog
program
mold
theater
flavor

How would Americans spell these words?

centre
defence
humour
levelled
manoeuvre

Probably the greatest English dictionary ever written was the great Oxford English Dictionary published in ten volumes between 1884 and 1928. This dictionary told the story of the changes in the meanings of words since they first appeared in print, how they were pronounced and all the uses of the words as recorded in many different books and newspapers. There were over five million quotations selected by eight hundred readers.

Find out the meanings of these words:

lexicographer   slang

Look up your dictionary to see if you can find these words:

hovercraft   videotape   aerospace
sit-in   splash-down

If you cannot find them, can you think why? If you can think of the right answer to this question, then where would you begin to look to find these words?

Can you find two or more meanings for these words?

canteen   list   mark   crash   maroon   palm

Can you work out from these definitions what the words are? To give you a clue, this group begins with **cas**:

An earthenware or oven-glass dish and lid, in which food can be cooked in an oven and brought on to the table.

Someone who has been wrecked on a desert island like Robinson Crusoe.

A small box, often beautifully decorated, in which jewels, love letters, etc., may be kept.

Here is another group, all beginning with **int**:

To be undamaged and all in one piece.
To be quick at understanding things.
Something that is done on purpose and not by accident.

Now try these, which all start with **prem**:

A feeling that something is about to happen.
Thought out beforehand.
Too soon; before the right time.

Here is a page from a children's dictionary. Examine it carefully.

What do the words *empty* and *evergreen* at the top of the page tell us?

empty   1. having nothing inside.
2. to take everything out of.

enamel   a hard bright paint or outer covering. Your teeth have a coating of *enamel*.

enchant   1. to fill with delight.
2. to cast a spell over.

enclose   to close or shut in: to put inside, especially to put inside a letter or its envelope.

encourage to give someone hope and courage to go on.

encyclopaedia a book or set of books giving facts on many different subjects.

enemy   someone or something fighting against you: a foe.

energy   force: power: activity.

engine   a machine in which energy is made to do work.

engineer   a man who understands *engines* and makes them go.

engulf   to swallow.—The great waves *engulfed* the swimmer.

enough   plenty: as much as is needed.

entertain to amuse in any way: to give pleasure to the mind. Television is a form of *entertainment*.

enthusiasm keen interest: eagerness to take part in some activity.

entire   whole: in one piece: all of anything.

entrance   the way in.

entry   1. a coming in: a way in.
2. an item written in a book, such as an *entry* in a diary.

envelope   a packet for sending letters through the post.

envy   1. a feeling of dislike or unhappiness at the good fortune of others.
2. to want something that belongs to others.

equal   to be the same. 8 is *equal* to $4 + 4$.

equator   an imaginary circle passing over the surface of the earth at an equal distance from the North and South Poles.

erect   1. standing straight up.
2. to build or set up.—The campers *erected* their tent.

err   to go astray: to make a mistake.

errand   a short trip to take a message or to fetch something.

fool's errand a wasted journey.

error   a slip or mistake.

erupt   to burst out, as a volcano does.

escape   to get away from danger.

eternal   everlasting.

evening   the time when day ends and night begins.

event   a happening.

evergreen a tree that has green leaves all the year round.

The words in the dictionary are listed in strict alphabetical order.

If we wished to put the word *evaporation* into our dictionary, between which two words would it go? Look up the meaning of *evaporation* in your own dictionary.

One of the things we learn from a dictionary is how to spell words.

Here is a list written out by a pupil. He was asked to spell ten words from this page of the dictionary. He has made three mistakes. Find the three words he has made mistakes in, and write them out correctly.

Tom Smith

1. errupt
2. envelope
3. encyclopaedia
4. equal
5. equater
6. enamel
7. enthusiasm
8. encourage
9. enginer
10. enough

The most important thing a dictionary tells us is the meaning of words.

Some words can have more than one meaning. It is then essential to choose the correct one.

What is the meaning of each of the words in italics in these sentences?

On the spot where the farm had stood a new block of flats had been *erected*.
Dr Johnson's dictionary contained about 40,000 *entries*.
The beautiful scenery quite *enchanted* the visitors.
He asked the child to *empty* the waste paper basket.

Some dictionaries contain illustrations. If you were asked to include the following illustrations in a dictionary page, beside which entries would you place them.

Making Your Own Dictionary

A useful way to learn about dictionaries is to make one of your own.

Any jotter will do. Give a double page to A, a double page to B, and so on.

Any new word you come across should be written in with its meaning under the appropriate letter.

Sometimes the meaning of a word is best explained by an illustration. In that case a picture or drawing should be pasted in.

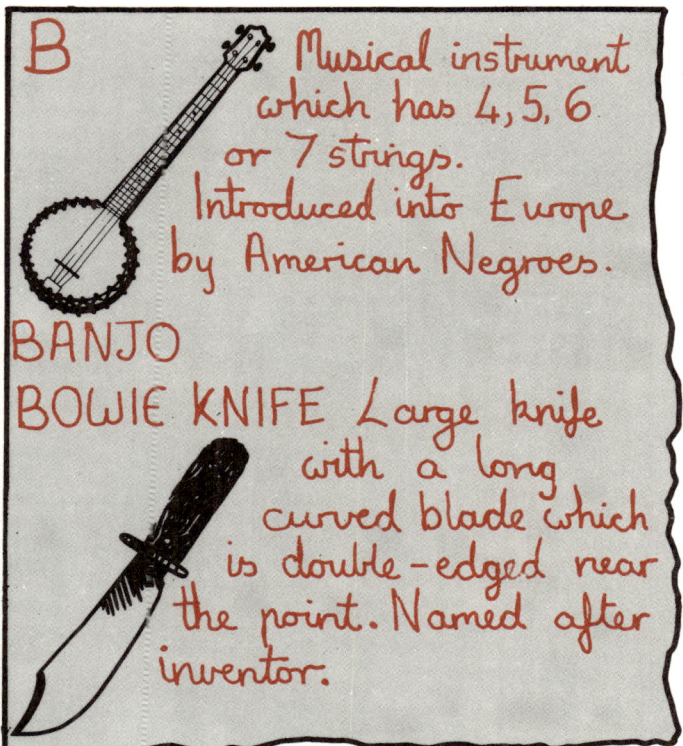

B

Musical instrument which has 4, 5, 6 or 7 strings. Introduced into Europe by American Negroes.

BANJO

BOWIE KNIFE Large knife with a long curved blade which is double-edged near the point. Named after inventor.

A page from your dictionary would probably look something like this.

Write down in your own words what astronomy means.

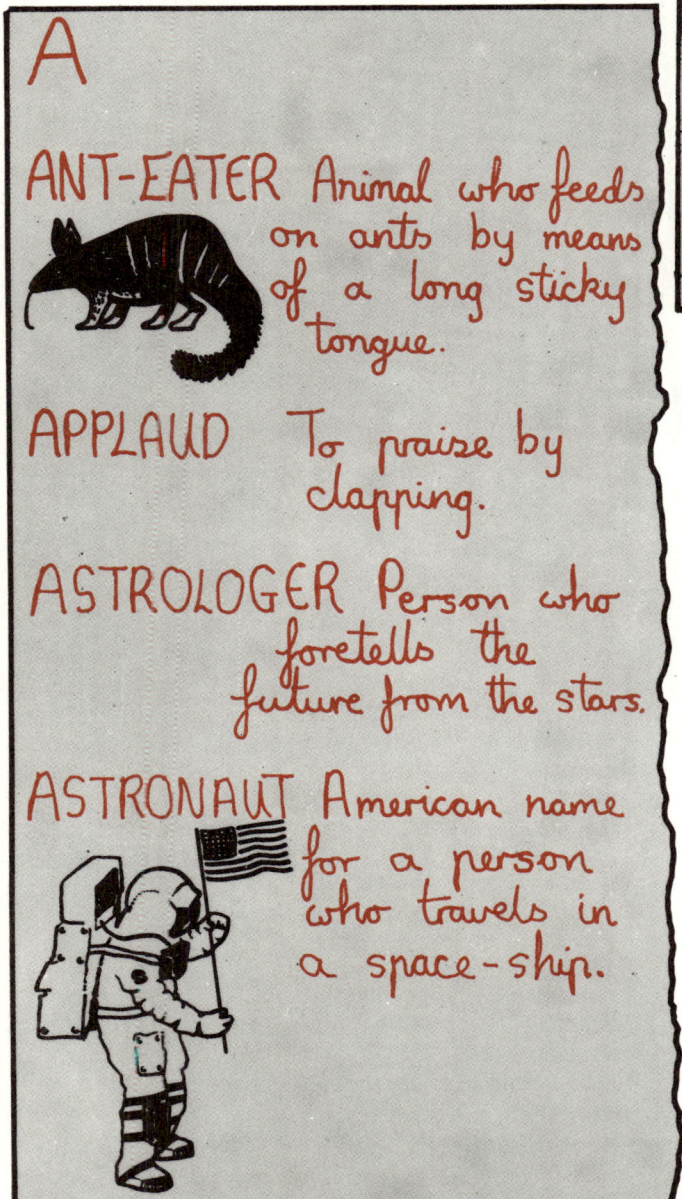

A

ANT-EATER Animal who feeds on ants by means of a long sticky tongue.

APPLAUD To praise by clapping.

ASTROLOGER Person who foretells the future from the stars.

ASTRONAUT American name for a person who travels in a space-ship.

The GIANT All-Colour DICTIONARY

Hamlyn

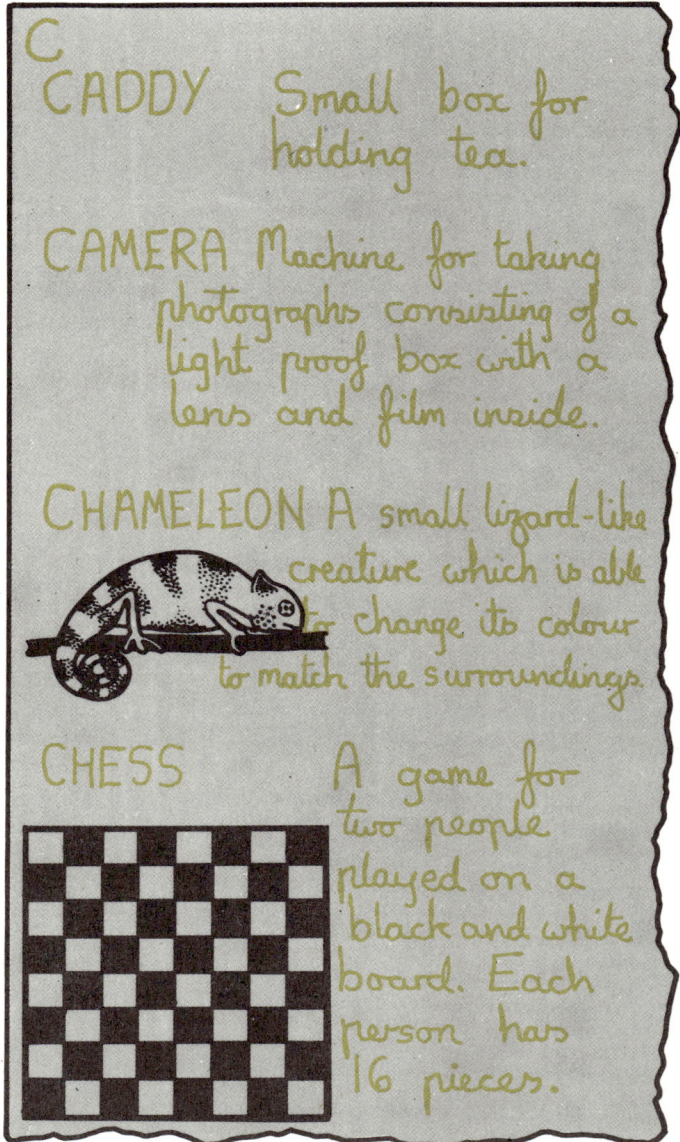

C

CADDY Small box for holding tea.

CAMERA Machine for taking photographs consisting of a light proof box with a lens and film inside.

CHAMELEON A small lizard-like creature which is able to change its colour to match the surroundings.

CHESS A game for two people played on a black and white board. Each person has 16 pieces.

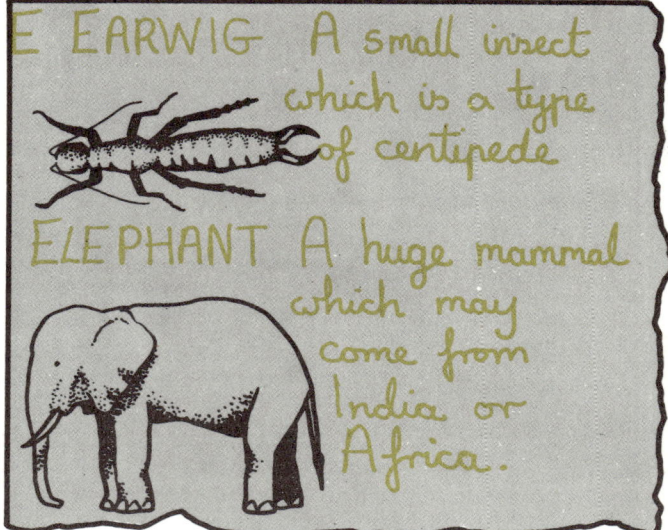

D

DHOW A lateen-rigged native boat used on the Arabian Sea.

DOLPHIN A mammal like a Porpoise but with a longer and more slender snout.

E EARWIG A small insect which is a type of centipede

ELEPHANT A huge mammal which may come from India or Africa.

Look up your dictionary and find the answer to the following clues.

The first two letters are given to help you. The number of dots show the number of missing letters.

Clue	Answer
A type of hymn	AN . . . .
What a ship carries to steady it when it has no cargo	BA . . . . .
To knit with a single hooked needle	CR . . . . .
One who attracts others into a trap	DE . . .
A river mouth	ES . . . . .
A mistaken idea	FA . . . .
A group of trees	GR . . .
Unfriendly	HO . . . .
To set fire to	IG . . . .
The fiftieth anniversary	JU . . . . .
A small bird of the hawk family	KI . .
A church reading desk	LE . . . . .
A sailor	MA . . . . .
Something new or unusual	NO . . . . .
Hateful and offensive	OD . . . .
A list of ancestors	PE . . . . .
Any four-footed animal	QU . . . .
A small piece left over after the rest has been used up	RE . . . .
A lightweight rowing boat	SK . . .
A cheap ornament	TR . . . . .
Result	UP . . . .
Poisonous	VE . . . . . .
A little beetle that damages food and crops	WE . . . .
A wooden frame put round the neck of oxen	YO . .
A scientist who studies animals	ZO . . . .

More Advanced Dictionaries

axe n. hatchet.

baa n. the noise made by a sheep [Imitation of sound].

baboon n. a large monkey with a long dog-like face [Fr. babouin].

bachelor n. an unmarried man; a person who has taken a degree at university.

back n. the opposite of front; one of the players behind the forwards in football.

bad adj. wicked, evil, not good.

bacon n. pig's flesh. To save one's bacon —to escape unharmed.

badge n. an emblem.

badger n. a burrowing animal; v. to pester, to worry.

bag n. a sack. Adj. *baggy*—loose. To let the cat out of the bag—to give away a secret.

bail n. money put up to allow an accused person to go free; one of two wooden cross pieces on the wicket at cricket.

BAILS

bairn n. a child [Scot.].

bake v. to cook, to prepare food in an oven.

baker n. one who bakes. Baker's dozen—thirteen.

balalaika n. a stringed musical instrument [Russian].

ball n. any round object; a dance.

balm (bahm) n. ointment.

balmoral n. a flat Scottish bonnet [From Balmoral, the royal castle in Aberdeenshire].

This is a more advanced dictionary and gives you more information than the dictionary on page 11.

If you wanted to include the word *baby* in our dictionary, between which two words would you put it?

If you wished to include *bait*, between which two words would it go?

One of the things which this dictionary tells us is what part of speech a word is.

If you look just after each word you will find n. (noun) or v. (verb) or adj. (adjective).

What part of speech are: *baboon, bake, baker*?

What does *badger* mean as a noun?

What does it mean as a verb?

What is the adjective from bag?

Sometimes under the same heading as the word we get phrases that come from the word.

What phrase do we find under the heading of *baker*?

What does *to save one's bacon* mean?

What phrase means *to give away a secret*?

Write down the correct meaning for each of the words in italic in the following sentences:

Cinderella went to the *ball*.

The bat knocked off a *bail*.

The left *back* is captain of the team.

His teacher is a *bachelor* of science.

The prisoner was told that *bail* would be £50.

Some of the information in a dictionary is given inside brackets.

Inside the round brackets ( ) in this dictionary we find how to pronounce difficult words.

In the word *balm* we find that the *l* is silent and we pronounce it as 'bahm', with a long a-sound, as in 'father'.

Inside the square brackets [ ] we find where the word first came from.

With *baa*, we learn that the word was just an attempt to imitate the sound a sheep makes.

Which word in our dictionary do we get from French?

Can you spot a Scottish word?

From which language does balalaika come?

What hat is named after a castle?

Write down TRUE or FALSE for each of the following sentences.

A *baboon* can be seen in the zoo.

We make tea in a *balalaika*.

A *baker's* dozen is more than twelve.

Bacon comes from a sheep.

More Things to Look Up in Your Dictionary

Write down the letter that is silent in each of these words:

> **subtle**
>
> **nestle**
>
> **character**
>
> **pneumonia**

From which languages do we get the following words?

lava
rucksack
blancmange
algebra
submarine
ski
amok
telephone
serviette
skipper

What is the origin of each of the following words?

galvanize
cuckoo
sardine
holiday
goodbye
volcano
penknife
cardigan
alphabet

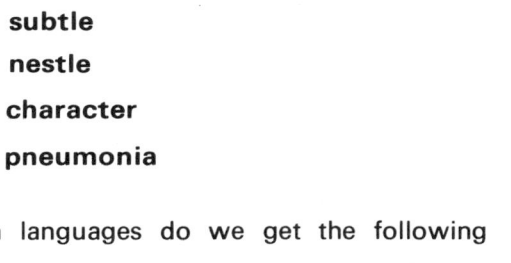

The italic words in the sentences below are all words that can have several meanings.

Use your dictionary to find the one correct meaning for each italic word.

The doctor warned him that the broken bone would *knit* very slowly.

It was a *novel* way of solving the problem.

He had a *rent* in his coat.

The position was very *grave*.

The man was caught in a traffic *jam*.

The *major* part of the work has already been done.

Write TRUE or FALSE after each of these statements.

An astronomer studies the stars.

An elver is a plant.

Tandem comes from a German word.

The rowan is another name for the mountain ash.

A palliasse is a type of carriage.

Encyclopædias

Look up the word *encyclopaedia* in your dictionary.

Go to the library and ask to see all the encyclopaedias on the shelves.

What do you think is the main difference between a dictionary and an encyclopaedia?

Now decide what an encyclopaedia tells you and when you will need to use it.

The Encyclopaedia Britannica is one of the most famous of all encyclopaedias.

- It was first printed in 1768 and since then there have been 15 completely new editions.

- In the latest edition there are 43 million words and 33,141 pages.

- It took 15 years to produce, and contains 18,425 photographs, 3,852 drawings, 1,174 maps, and 160 colour plates.

- The publishers employed 4,277 writers from 131 countries.

This is a caricature—a comic drawing—of the two men responsible for the first edition of the *Encyclopaedia Britannica*. They are Andrew Bell (left) its engraver and one of its publishers and William Smellie, the Edinburgh scholar who was its editor. The picture was drawn by John Kay in 1757.

Here is a set of the modern Encyclopaedia Britannica.

But of course there are many encyclopaedias. It is strange to think that one of the oldest and best-known was published by a soap manufacturer—Pears' Encyclopaedia.

Why should a manufacturer of soap want to publish an encyclopaedia?

A hundred years ago very many people were unable to read. But as more children went to school, more and more readers wanted to learn about history, geography, science and other subjects. An encyclopaedia in your own home was a great help in finding out about these things.

Which of these words would you look up in a dictionary and which in an encyclopaedia?

Shakespeare	**Paris**
Perhaps	**Stagger**
Canada	**Healthy**

Pears' soap

PEARS
CYCLOPAEDIA 80th EDITION

HARPOON

From earliest times some form of harpoon has been used in fishing. It is a spear with a special barbed end, which sticks firmly in the flesh of the fish. The other end of the spear usually has a cord, which enables the owner to pull it back to him after it has been thrown. The harpoons used in whaling are shot from powerful guns.

Codes. When a message is to be sent to somebody and its meaning is to be kept a secret, a code is often used. There is no end to the ways a code may be constructed. Here is a simple message in code. Can you find out what it says?

GSRH RH DIRGGVM RM XLWV.

Before you can read the message you must discover the code. It consists merely in writing the alphabet from A to Z in a horizontal line. Then, in a line below the first, the alphabet is again written, but this time it is set down backwards. Thus Z is A, Y is B, X is C, and so on until A is Z. Now you will be able to read the message.

Willett, William (1856-1915). The man who first suggested that we should have "Summer Time", or, as it is sometimes called, "Daylight Saving". Unfortunately, he never knew what it was like to put the clocks forward and have an extra hour's daylight in the evenings, because he died in 1915 and the scheme was started in 1916. (See **Summer Time.**)

VENICE

"The Queen of the Adriatic" is the name given to this beautiful city in Italy* at the north of the Adriatic Sea. Venice is built entirely on islands. Instead of streets it has many canals and people travel by gondola or, more cheaply, by waterbus.

For several centuries, Venice was the greatest maritime power in the world. Ruled by the Doge (chief magistrate), she controlled the overland trade with the East and sent her galleys throughout the Mediterranean and to England, Flanders and the Baltic. Her merchants and their navies transported the Crusaders, fought the Turks, and Venice's rivals at Genoa.

The power of Venice started to decline when the Turks conquered the eastern Mediterranean lands and a new route was found by sea to the East. But her wealth had given her the most splendid buildings and palaces in Europe.

Excalibur: the great sword of King Arthur that 'gave light like thirty torches'. In the Arthurian stories, the name is given to two different swords— the one that the young king pulled from the anvil set in the stone before the church, and so proved his right to the kingship; and the other which the king took from the arm that rose above the surface of the lake, 'clothed in white samite, mystic, wonderful' and which eventually received back the sword when Arthur was dying.

On this page you can see extracts from several well-known encyclopaedias.

They show the wide variety of information an encyclopaedia gives.

What finally happened to King Arthur's sword, Excalibur?

Who first suggested Daylight Saving?

By what title was the chief magistrate of Venice known?

When is a code used?

What is the main difference between an ordinary harpoon and the harpoon used in whaling?

Cross References

These are references to other sections of the encyclopaedia. They tell you what to look up if you want to know more about a certain subject.

Find all the cross references in the extracts opposite. What are some of the ways cross references are shown?

Which cross reference should you follow up if you wish to understand a little more about

William Willett?   Venice?

With the help of your own encyclopaedia write a short encyclopaedia extract on

Daylight Saving   King Arthur

Volumes

Since an encyclopaedia tries to give information about almost every subject it is usually a very big book. Very often it is so big, in fact, that all the information will not go into one book. It has to be put into several books, or *volumes*. (The word 'volume' comes to us from the Romans. Try looking it up in your dictionary. See if you can find what it originally meant.)

Here are some well-known children's encylopaedias on a library bookshelf.

If you look at the volumes in the illustration carefully you will see that they are all numbered.

Even before you take it down from the shelf, each volume tells you something about the subjects in it, usually by alphabetical order. For example, the Children's Britannica, Volume 12 covers things whose names come in the spelling group *moth* to *oyster*. Black's Children's Encyclopaedia is in two volumes, one for each half of the alphabet. The Oxford Junior Encyclopaedia is divided into subjects —for instance 'Plants' come under 'Natural History' in Volume 2. But there is also a long index to help you and it takes up the whole of Volume 13. We shall discuss indexes in the next chapter

Below are some encyclopaedias of a different kind.

Here is a list of subjects that you could find in the three encyclopaedias shown above. Sort them into three groups, one belonging to each book.

Hannibal
Glaciers
The Emperor Claudius
The American War of Independence
The French Revolution
Fossils

Early civilizations
Sedimentary rocks
The First World War
Darius the Great
Gold
William Pitt

What is the main difference between this kind of encyclopaedia and all the others we have been discussing up till now?

Can you think of any other one-subject encyclopaedias?

Name a few subjects on which you would like to have encyclopaedias.

Go to your school library or local library and see if any encyclopaedias actually exist on any of these subjects.

Using your Encyclopaedia

The answers to all the following questions can be found in your encyclopaedia.

The word to look up for each question is printed in italics.

What part of *Achilles* was not dipped in the River Styx?

Who invented the method of printing which helps blind people to read, and which we call *Braille*?

To which country did *Confucius* belong?

We say "as dead as a dodo". What is or was a *Dodo*?

Which two different kinds of *Elephant* are found in the world?

What did Henry *Ford* do?

When is St *George's* day?

Name any work written by the composer *Handel*.

Where did the *Incas* live?

From which part of the world do *Jaguars* come?

What is made from *Kaolin*?

What was the full name of *Lawrence* of *Arabia*?

Who signed *Magna Carta*?

Write one sentence about *Nitrogen*.

Where were the first *Olympic Games* held? ·

What was *Pegasus*?

By what name is *Quicksilver* now known?

Which country invented the *Rocket* during the Middle Ages?

Who beat Captain *Scott* to the South Pole?

In which war was the *Tank* first used?

When was the *United Nations Organisation (U.N.O.)* founded?

Who were the original *Vandals*?

To which modern country would you travel to see the battlefield of *Waterloo*?

Can you name the man who discovered *X-Rays*?

By what name did the Romans call *York*?

Who or what was *Zeus*?

Table of Contents and Index

Other types of encyclopaedia do not list their subjects in alphabetical order, but put them instead into sections. So the facts about Armour and Swords, which you can find on pages 92 and 93 of Macmillan's Our World Encyclopaedia, Volume 1, belong to the section on Warfare.

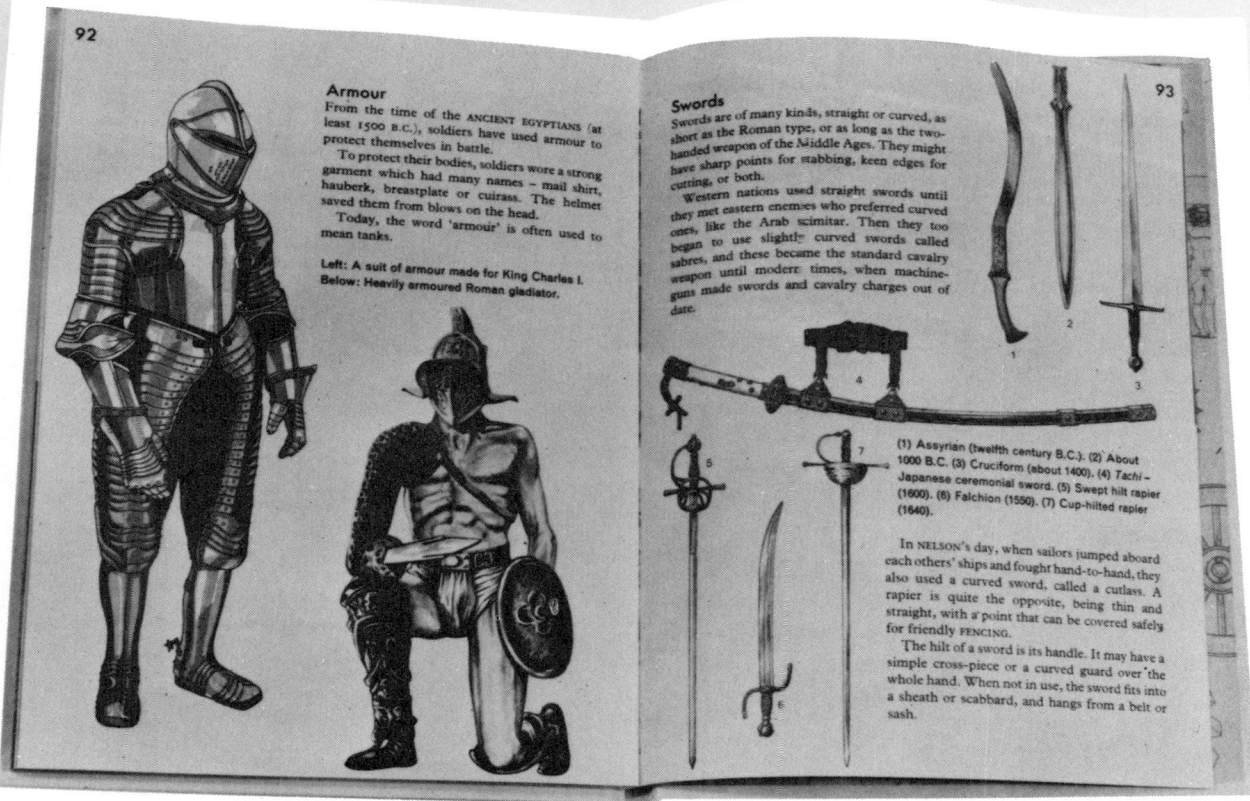

92

Armour
From the time of the ANCIENT EGYPTIANS (at least 1500 B.C.), soldiers have used armour to protect themselves in battle.

To protect their bodies, soldiers wore a strong garment which had many names – mail shirt, hauberk, breastplate or cuirass. The helmet saved them from blows on the head.

Today, the word 'armour' is often used to mean tanks.

Left: A suit of armour made for King Charles I.
Below: Heavily armoured Roman gladiator.

Swords
93

Swords are of many kinds, straight or curved, as short as the Roman type, or as long as the two-handed weapon of the Middle Ages. They might have sharp points for stabbing, keen edges for cutting, or both.

Western nations used straight swords until they met eastern enemies who preferred curved ones, like the Arab scimitar. Then they too began to use slightly curved swords called sabres, and these became the standard cavalry weapon until modern times, when machine-guns made swords and cavalry charges out of date.

(1) Assyrian (twelfth century B.C.). (2) About 1000 B.C. (3) Cruciform (about 1400). (4) *Tachi* – Japanese ceremonial sword. (5) Swept hilt rapier (1600). (6) Falchion (1550). (7) Cup-hilted rapier (1640).

In NELSON's day, when sailors jumped aboard each others' ships and fought hand-to-hand, they also used a curved sword, called a cutlass. A rapier is quite the opposite, being thin and straight, with a point that can be covered safely for friendly FENCING.

The hilt of a sword is its handle. It may have a simple cross-piece or a curved guard over the whole hand. When not in use, the sword fits into a sheath or scabbard, and hangs from a belt or sash.

TABLE OF CONTENTS

Here is the first page of another encyclopaedia of this type.

As you can see, this is its Table of Contents—a list of what appears in the various chapters.

Which chapter would you look up if you wanted information on these subjects?

your heart

rugby

King Richard the Lionheart of England

your favourite T.V. programme

railways

the man who discovered Australia

Eskimos

who invented the radio

Picasso, the painter

Marconi at the age of twenty-two.

Index

Although the entries in some encyclopaedias are not arranged alphabetically, there is an alphabetical list at the end which we call the index. The index lists all the subjects dealt with and gives you the page on which each is mentioned.

Here is a page from an index.

Roundheads 69
Royal Air Force 87, 326
Royal Standard 159
Rubens, P 289
rugby 189
Russia 87, 150

sailing ships 304
St Andrew 147
St George 146
sand lizard 138
Saxon kings 62
Schubert, F. 291
Scots 38, 62, 150
Scott, Capt. R. 348
Scott, Terry 222
Scott, Sir W. 252–254

sea horse 101
seaplane 327
Second World War 199–200
senses 49
Shakespeare, W. 69, 241–243
Shaw, G. B. 270
Shelley, P. B. 262
ships 310–315
shoulders 47
shrew 129
signal box 329
singing 294–300
skeleton 45
skin 48
snail 128
snakes 130
Snow White 220

As you can see, an index is very handy for finding what you are looking for in a book.

If you want information about "seaplanes", you look it up under the letter S in the index and find out that seaplanes are mentioned on page 327.

You then read page 327 and get your information.

On which page would you find information about these?

the sand lizard   Roundheads

the Royal Standard

Snow White   Franz Schubert

Using Both The Index And The Table Of Contents

On which page is St George mentioned?

Which chapter of the book is that? (Check from your "Table of Contents").

The R.A.F. is mentioned on page 87 and page 326. Which two chapters are these?

By using your Index and Table of Contents find out in which three chapters the Scots are mentioned.

By using your Index and Table of Contents can you guess the occupation or job of

Scott, Capt. R. ?   Scott, Sir W. ?

Scott, Terry ?

Remember that many other books have an index as well. Try these questions to see how much you have learned about the use of the index.

If you were looking up Charles Dickens in an index would you look under "C" or under "D"?

Write down your own name as it would appear in an index.

If you saw the following entry in an index—Smith, J. 6, 83–84, 101—it would mean that J. Smith was mentioned in three different places in the book.

Which one would you look up first?

Why would you look this one up first?

Finding a Poem in an Index

If you are looking for a certain poem in a poetry book you can, of course, start at the beginning and thumb your way right through the book.

This is a very slow and time-wasting method.

A much easier way to find a poem in a poetry book is to use the index.

Here the poems are usually listed under the names of the poets. These names are arranged in alphabetical order.

Here is a typical poetry book index:

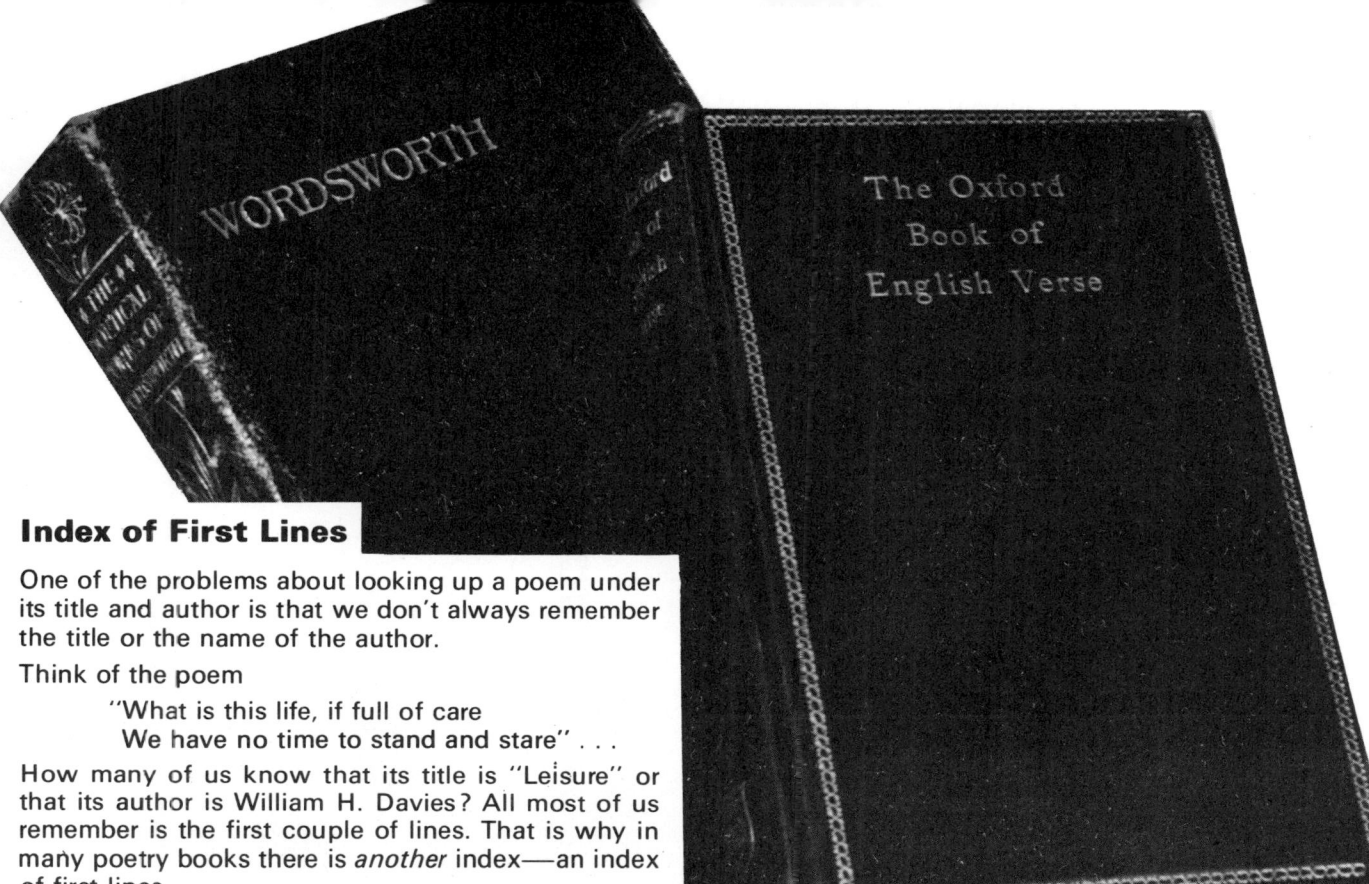

Index of First Lines

One of the problems about looking up a poem under its title and author is that we don't always remember the title or the name of the author.

Think of the poem

> "What is this life, if full of care
> We have no time to stand and stare" . . .

How many of us know that its title is "Leisure" or that its author is William H. Davies? All most of us remember is the first couple of lines. That is why in many poetry books there is *another* index—an index of first lines.

Here is an example of such an index.

By comparing the two indexes on Pages 30 and 31, find the titles of the poems of which these are the first lines.

The sun was shining on the sea

Head the ship for England

When I sailed out of Baltimore

Toll for the brave

Tom Pearse, Tom Pearse, lend me your grey mare

There are twelve months in all the year

It fell about the Martinmas time

Hamelin Town's in Brunswick

On Linden, when the sun was low

When Robin Hood and Little John

Good-bye, good-bye to summer

There was a youth, and a well-beloved youth.

What does 'Anonymous' mean? It can't really be an author's name—unless he was somebody who wrote a great deal! Look up this word in your dictionary and find out what it means and which language it comes from.

The Walrus and the Carpenter—from Lewis Carroll's Through the Looking Glass.

A statue of the poet Robert Burns, 1759–1796.

Give the first line of one of his poems. (See Page 31).

What can PICTURES tell you?

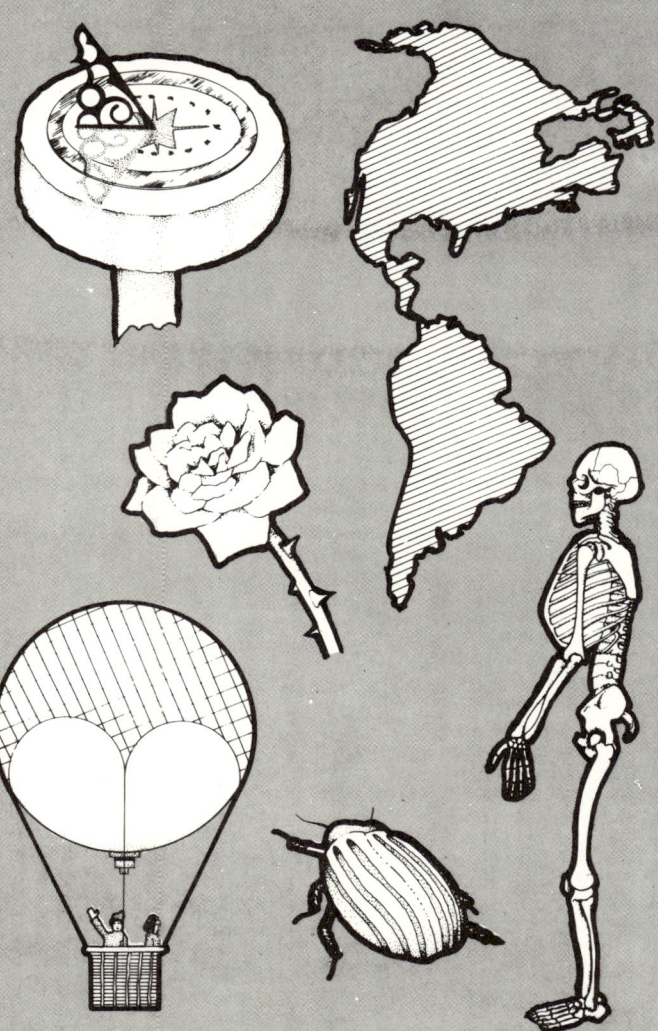

As you go looking for information you realize that pictures often play a big part.

Start by looking at the pictures on this page.

Can you write a sentence about each?

Look the word up in any encyclopaedia.

Make a few notes on what you found out.

'One picture is worth a thousand words'

Do you think there is any truth in this old Chinese saying?

Many reference books have pictures that help to make their meaning much clearer. Always take a careful look at the pictures, whether they are photographs, drawings or diagrams. They can help you to understand the subject better and give you a good grasp of the details. Try looking up some of the following, and study any illustrations you can find:

armadillo   Grand Canyon
Sydney Harbour Bridge   mosaic   iceberg
pyramid   Gothic architecture   cog wheel
dragonfly   power station   the coast of Britain

Now collect a few pictures from newspapers or magazines. You might choose, for example, a camera, a famous building, a well-known statesman, an animal or bird. Write your own description of each subject, as though you were compiling an encyclopaedia. Which is better—looking at the picture, or reading the words of explanation? Or is it better still to have both together?

Old and New Pictures

Sometimes old pictures look quaint and funny. But remember they can be immensely valuable in telling us how people lived in earlier times. Learn to look at old paintings and drawings. You will find out how people used to dress, how they built their houses, how they worked, how they travelled about and how they fought their wars.

The Bayeux Tapestry was made in needlework by Queen Matilda and her ladies at the time of the Norman Conquest in 1066. It is full of amazing details of ships, clothes, armour and animals—even though it does not quite fit in with modern ideas of perspective!

though it does not quite fit in with modern ideas of perspective!

Take a good look at this picture. A great deal is happening and this is the thick of the Battle of Hastings. The words in Latin say 'Harold the King was killed'.

Can you find Harold?

What can you discover about the type of armour and weapons used at this time?

Do you think there are any similarities between this tapestry and a modern strip cartoon?

The picture entitled 'The Bank' is actually a scene near the Bank of England. You could work out roughly at what date it was drawn. Was it one hundred years ago? Or two hundred? Or three or four hundred years ago? There are enough clues in the picture to tell you. Look at the clothes the people are wearing. Then study the style of architecture of the buildings.

Old photographs, too, may take you back a hundred years or more. The camera is a faithful recorder and it captures history while it is actually happening. Spend some time studying any old photographs you can find, and old sketches, cartoons and newspaper pictures also. Look closely at fashions in dress, look at background details and try to imagine yourself actually there and joining in the life of those times.

A Wright type bi-plane, 1910.

Find out first what the word 'biplane' means. Then look up the name 'Wright' in an encyclopaedia. There were two brothers of this name. What were they famous for? How much can you discover about them, and the early days of flying?

Look up in your encyclopaedia:

**Zeppelin Airship Lindbergh Blériot
Royal Flying Corps**

The photograph on this page shows a nineteenth century threshing scene where a flail is being used. Can you find out how a flail would separate the grain from the chaff? What is used today on a modern farm? Look at the barn and try to decide how it was built and guess how old it might be. Look at the people and their clothes. They may give you a clue about when the photograph was taken. Who do you think the people might be? Do you think some of them are from the same family? Imagine you are one of the children and describe what you can see and what you are thinking about.

Do you like cartoons? People have enjoyed cartoons for many years. Here is a seaside scene drawn about 1870. Look at the bathing dresses. How would the swimmers be dressed today? Which you do think is better for swimming? The strange-looking carts are called bathing machines. Find out all you can about them.

AWKWARD.

Modest Old Gentleman (who has swum out to sea, and whose bathing-machine has, in the meanwhile, been walked off by mistake). "AHEM! PRAY EXCUSE ME, MADAM! MY BATHING-MACHINE, I THINK."

In our own time, events are constantly being recorded, on newsreel and in newspaper photographs. Find pictures of some of the greatest happenings of recent years, and other pictures typical of the life we live today—school, work, shopping, amusements, holidays, travel, for instance, and say why they may interest historians two hundred years from now.

Facts and Figures in Picture Form

Sometimes the pictures in reference books are of this type:

This picture shows the proportion of black people to white people in South Africa. Each little figure stands for a quarter-of-a-million people.

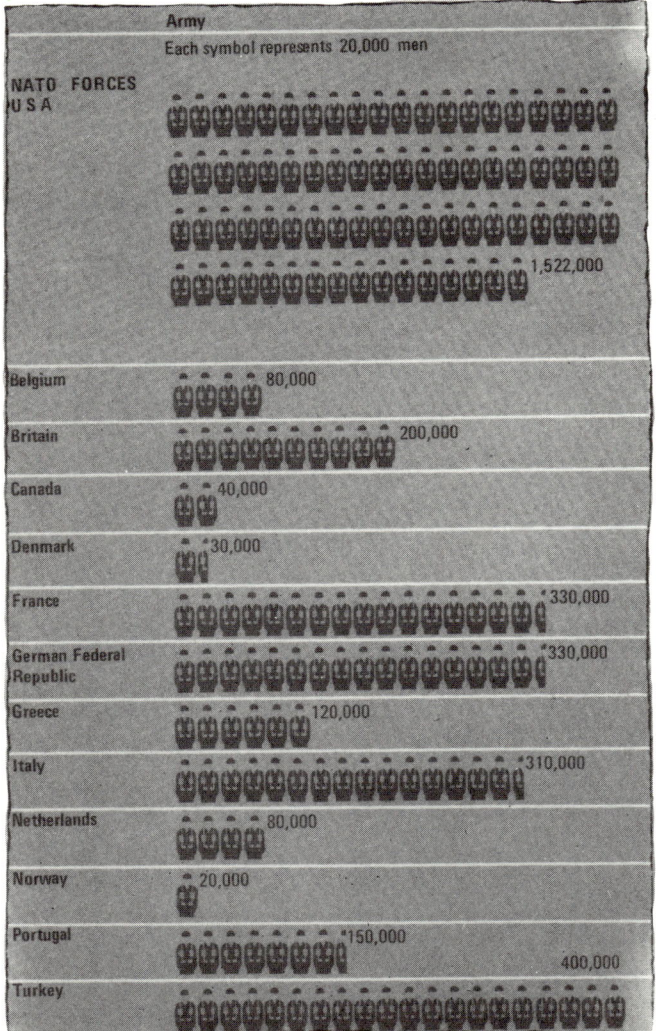

This picture shows the sizes of the armies of the various countries in the NATO alliance. Each drawing of a soldier represents 20,000 men.

Pictures like this, where each little human figure represents a certain number of people, are known as *pictographs*.

How many white people live in South Africa?

Which country has the second largest army in the NATO alliance?

Pictographs can be of many different kinds.

This picture shows the number of boys and girls at a school.

How many girls are there? How many boys are there?

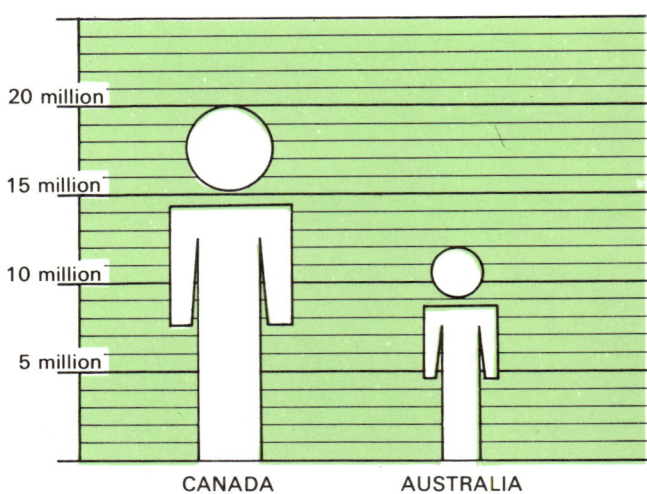

This picture illustrates the difference in population between Canada and Australia.

Which has the larger population?

What is the population of Canada?

Now draw your own pictographs to show:

A class which has 30 girls and 20 boys in it.
The population of Hong Kong (4 million), New Zealand (3 million) and Jamaica (2 million).

Graphs

With statistics—the technical name for collected facts and figures, such as those which governments use—a quick way of comparing a set of different figures is to show them as bars of different lengths. This bar graph shows you at a glance which of the world's major cities has the largest population at four different periods of history—1800, 1850, 1900 and 1930.

Has London always had more people than New York?

Which city increased its population fastest between 1900 and 1930?

Which city has shown the biggest increase in 130 years?

You probably recognize the type of graph which here shows unemployment figures. The same method is used, for example, to show rainfall for different months of the year, or somebody's temperature on different days.

In which year between 1926 and 1939 were there most people out of work, (a) in Britain, (b) in the U.S.A.?

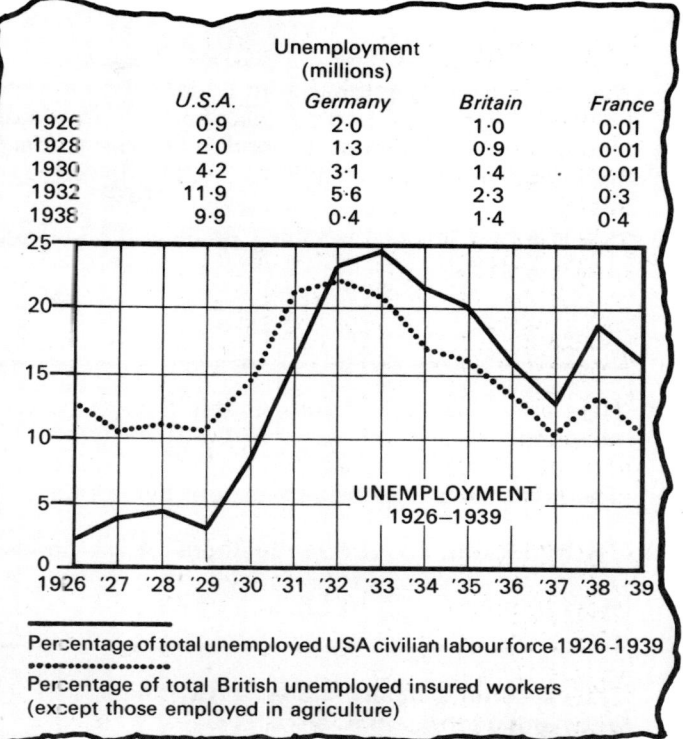

	U.S.A.	Germany	Britain	France
1926	0·9	2·0	1·0	0·01
1928	2·0	1·3	0·9	0·01
1930	4·2	3·1	1·4	0·01
1932	11·9	5·6	2·3	0·3
1938	9·9	0·4	1·4	0·4

Unemployment (millions)

UNEMPLOYMENT 1926–1939

——— Percentage of total unemployed USA civilian labour force 1926-1939

••••••••• Percentage of total British unemployed insured workers (except those employed in agriculture)

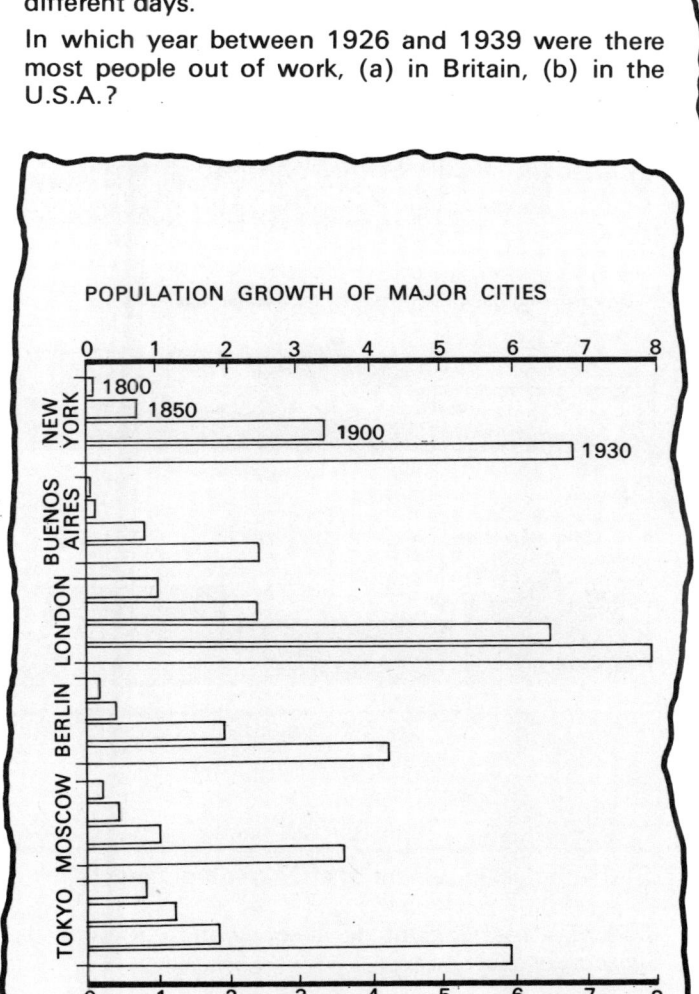

POPULATION GROWTH OF MAJOR CITIES

NEW YORK · BUENOS AIRES · LONDON · BERLIN · MOSCOW · TOKYO

1800 · 1850 · 1900 · 1930

(Population in millions)

Pie Diagrams

Another useful way in which figures are shown is by drawing a circle to represent a "pie". Then the pie is sliced up into portions to show how it is shared out.

Here is one of these diagrams showing how the world's output of hens' eggs is divided between different countries.

Which single country has the largest number of eggs?

Which country has the smallest?

Which has more eggs—West Germany or Japan?

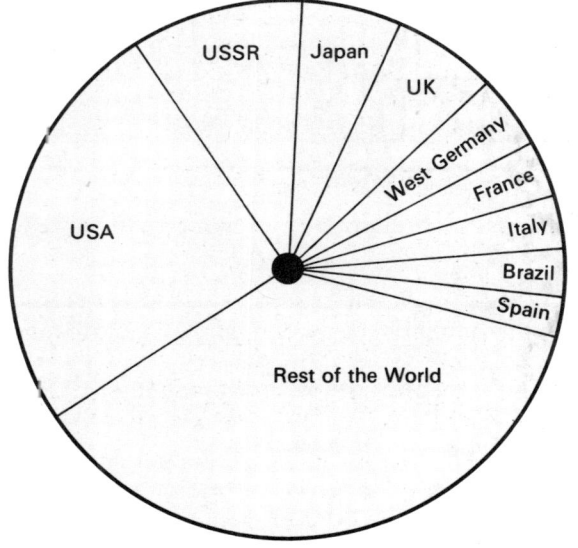

How-Things-Work Diagrams

Many things are much easier to understand with the help of a diagram. Often to describe them in words alone would take a long time and at the end you still might not have a very clear idea of what they were all about.

This diagram of hand weaving quickly lets you see how it is done.

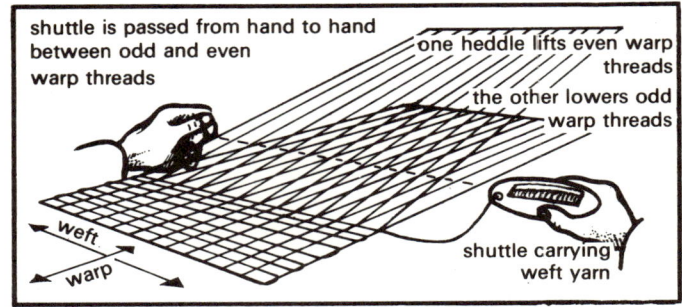

Here are some more diagrams, this time to do with shipping.

The first shows how fish are caught by a drifter.

Try to find out about other methods of fishing also.

How is a drifter different from a trawler?

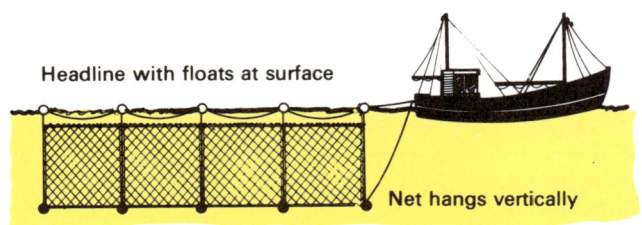

The second picture shows how ships can go downstream through a lock.

Can you draw another set of pictures to show how it would go upstream through a lock?

The working of a pound lock.

1 Both gates closed: ship waiting to enter

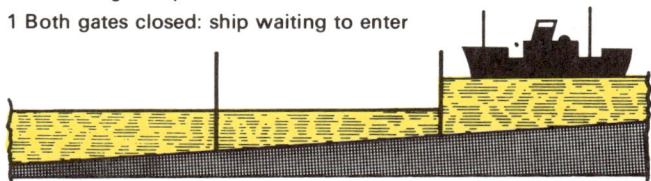

2 Upstream gate open; level of lock water rises

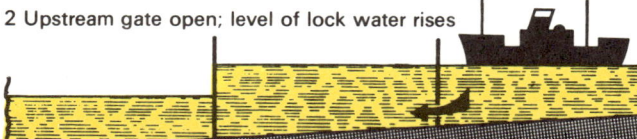

3 Both gates closed: ship now in the lock

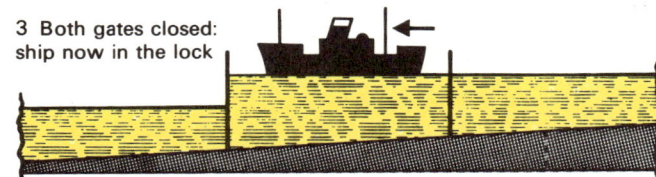

4 Downstream gate open: level of lock water falls

5 Ship leaves lock: return to Stage 1

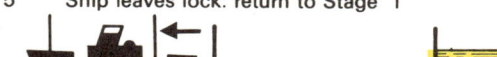
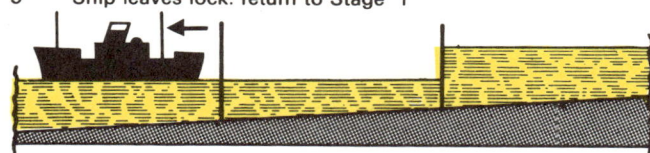

Now try some descriptions of your own, and use diagrams to help you.

Explain the difference between *concave* and *convex*.

Give a short account of the art of *heraldry*.

Explain what a *spiral staircase* is.

Show the development of a *tadpole* from egg to frog.

Describe the ancient form of writing known as *hieroglyphic writing*.

Give a description with illustrations of the *phases of the moon*.

BIOGRAPHICAL DICTIONARIES

A biographical dictionary gives brief details of the lives of famous people from the past.

Look up *biography* in your dictionary.
Look up *autobiography*.

Below are six drawings of famous people from the past. Beneath them are six names.

Match the correct names with the correct drawings.

Now write one sentence about each person.

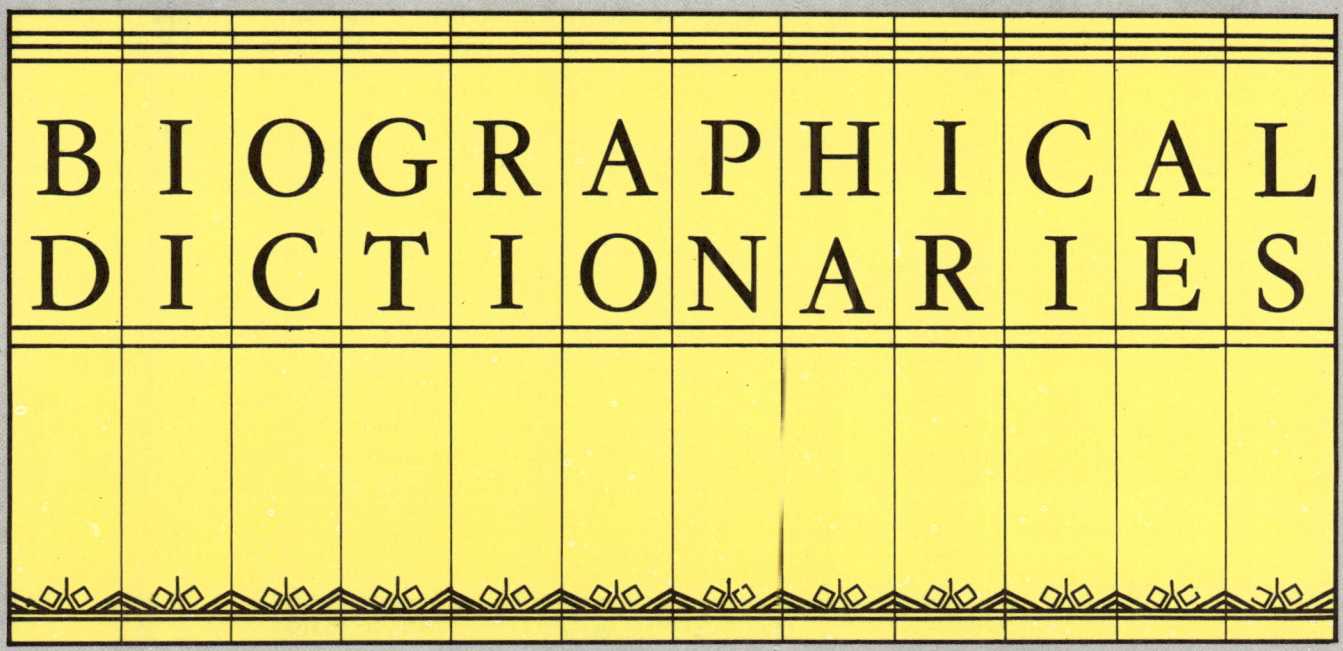

Julius Caesar, Napoleon Bonaparte, Adolf Hitler, General Custer, Joan of Arc, Abraham Lincoln

John XXIII (1881–1963)

He became Pope in succession to Pope Pius XII in 1958. Although he was only Pope for five years he became a very popular figure among people of many religions. He made strenuous efforts for world peace and Christian unity, and his death in 1963 was mourned all over the world.

Johnson, Amy (1903–1941)

Born in Hull in England, Amy Johnson became one of the early female pioneers in flying. In 1930 she became the first woman to fly single-handed from London to Australia. During the war she became a ferry pilot for the R.A.F., but she was killed in an air crash in 1941.

Johnson, Samuel (1709–1784)

A country schoolmaster, Samuel Johnson came to London to become a writer. Much of his writing was for the magazines of the period, but his greatest work was undoubtedly his "Dictionary of the English Language", which established him as one of the greatest scholars of his time and was used as a model by all later dictionary writers.

John the Baptist

John the Baptist was a cousin of Jesus and was born only six months before Him. He spent much of his life preparing the way for Jesus, preaching and baptising in the wilderness around Jordan. He objected publicly to the second marriage of King Herod Antipas and made an enemy of his second wife. When Salome danced for the king he promised her whichever reward she cared to ask for, and, spurred on by the king's second wife, she asked for the head of John the Baptist. John was duly beheaded and his head presented to Salome.

In a biographical dictionary the names of the famous people are listed in alphabetical order. Above is a page from a biographical dictionary.

What did Amy Johnson achieve in 1930?

What job did Samuel Johnson have before he came to London?

Who was the Pope before John XXIII?

To whose marriage did John the Baptist object?

Who

was a pilot?

wrote a dictionary?

prepared the way for Jesus?

worked to achieve Christian unity?

was beheaded?

If all the people in our page from the biographical dictionary were still alive today, who would be the youngest? Who would be the oldest?
Who lived longer—Samuel Johnson or John XXIII?
Only two could possibly have met. Which two?

Here are some famous people. Put them into alphabetical order, find out a little about six of them Write them down as a page in a biographical dictionary.

Winston Churchill
Canaletto
Miguel de Cervantes
Lewis Carroll
Sebastian Cabot
Thomas Telford
Cecil Rhodes
Florence Nightingale
Queen Victoria
William Penn
Marie Curie
Marco Polo
Paul Kruger
Mahatma Gandhi
Marie Antoinette
Toussaint L'Ouverture
Simon Bolivar
William Booth

Paul Kruger

William Penn

WHO'S WHO?

There is a type of reference book called *Who's Who* which gives details of the lives of famous people who are still living, or were alive at the time the book was published.

Here are four famous people from various walks of life.

Write down the name of each, then write a few sentences about each one.

Famous People

The original *Who's Who* is an extremely large book which gives details of people in all walks of life. Below is a typical page from *Who's Who*.

BASS, George; M.P. (Lab) Warrender West since 1945; Journalist and War Correspondent; b. 17th October, 1919; s. of J. Bass, Newcastle-Upon-Tyne; m. 1940 Martha, d. of G. Greenshields, London; two d. Educ; John Gray High School; Trinity College, Cambridge (B.A. 1940). Journalist and war correspondent in Asia and Western Europe, 1940–45. Publications: A War Correspondent's Diary, 1946; Strategy for Europe, 1954; The Common Market Dilemma, 1968. Recreations: reading, travel, golf, chess. Address: Westview, Warrender, Lincs. T: Warrender 317.

BARR, Laurence John; actor; b. 21st May 1917, son of the late Rev. S. S. Barr and Susan Graham Miller, m. 1st 1938 Agnes Robertson (divorced 1941); one s., 2nd 1941 Edna Thacker; Educ. Eton, Oxford (M.A. 1938). First appeared on stage 1934 with Liverpool Repertory Company, Hamlet at Old Vic, 1939; First film "Last Train To Tokyo", 1943; other roles include Othello, the sergeant in "War Over The Pacific", Malvolio in "Twelfth Night", and his Oscar-winning role in the film "Blue Rose". Recreations: golf, mountaineering, ski-ing. Clubs: Garrick, Green Room.

BARTON, Herbert Jones, O.B.E. (1930); author; b. Cardiff, 24th April, 1899, m. 1924, Anna, y.d. of the late Major J. Gibson, M.C.; two s. Educ. Cardiff High; Magdalen College, Oxford (B.A. 1922); 2nd Lieutenant 1st Lancs Regt, 1917, Capt. 1918; Music critic Daily Clarion, 1923–24, literary critic Daily Gazette, 1925–27. Publications: Poems, 1927; Death in the Desert, 1928; Rope Ladder, 1930; History of the French Revolution, 1935; Yellow Heaven, 1943; A New Beginning, 1953; Old Men Remember, 1969. Recreations: fishing, reading, travel. Clubs: Savile, Press.

BASLIE, Graham Symington; Professor of Germanic Languages, Univ. of Lisbourne; b. Glasgow, 13th February, 1910, s. of Prof. J. Baslie and Elizabeth Morton; m. 1939 Jessie, d. of Rev. J. Bell, Dundee; three s. Educ. Lanark Grammar, Univ. of St Andrews (M.A. 1932); Univ. of Cologne (Ph.D., 1936); Lecturer in German, Univ. of Durham, 1936–48; Senior Lecturer in Germanic Languages, Univ. of Lisbourne, 1948–64. Publications: The Romantic Revival in German Literature, 1936; Schiller, A New Approach, 1948. Recreations: music, fishing. Address: 2, University Avenue, Lisbourne.

For which film did Laurence Barr win an Oscar?

What job did George Bass have before he became an M.P.?

Which school did H. J. Barton attend?

Who married the daughter of an army officer?

At which German university did Professor Baslie study?

What is the main difference between a biographical dictionary and *Who's Who*?

If you were organizing a golf match, which two of the people from our page of *Who's Who* would you invite?

If you were arranging a day's fishing which two would you include?

Who is the eldest of the four?

Who is the youngest?

Which one had the largest family?

Which two studied at the same university?

Draw an envelope and address it to Graham Baslie.

Which two don't give an address?

How would you get in touch with them if you wished to write to them?

> *Something To Do*
> Choose three of your schoolfriends.
> Imagine that it is forty years on and they have all become famous.
> Write brief biographies for them as they might appear in a future edition of *Who's Who*.

Among the *Who's Who* type of reference books are special books dealing with the lives and achievements of people in certain professions and occupations.

Examples of this type of reference book are *Who's Who in Football*, *Who's Who in Parliament*, *Who's Who in Cricket*, *Who's Who in Acting*, *Who's Who in Business*, etc. There is even a book called *Who Was Who!*

In what sort of book would you find details about the following?

Gary Sobers
Elizabeth Taylor
Jim Slater
Jeremy Thorpe
Sir Alf Ramsey
Joe Frazier
Sir Laurence Olivier
Michael Foot
Lord Sieff
Glenda Jackson
Don Revie
Margaret Thatcher

Look through your daily paper and pick out:

two famous names on the sports pages
two famous names on the business pages
two famous names on the news pages.

Now see what you can find out about them from books, magazines and other newspapers.

If you were to be given a *Who's Who* type of reference book, on which subject would you like it to be? Give six names you would like to see in it.

Kissinger's Rescue Mission

ALISTAIR MACLEAN'S 21st

Yamani relives escape

Vorster's troops quit

THE YEHUDI MENUHIN *Music Guides*

Famous Figures in Football

Here are typical entries that you might find in a book dealing with one particular sport:

SAMMY McILROY—Manchester United

Joining United as a school-leaver, Sammy's big chance came when Denis Law was injured and he replaced the star in a local derby clash. The date was November 6th, 1971 and the match was against Manchester City at Maine Road. This was Sammy's first season as a professional and he scored in a 3-3 draw. In his next match he scored once again. After that he frequently played in the United side.

He was selected for the Northern Ireland side for the match against Spain in 1972. He had to drop out of football half-way through the 1972–3 season when he was injured in a car crash.

FRANK McLINTOCK—Queen's Park Rangers
Born in Glasgow on December 28th, 1939, Frank is 5 ft 9½ in tall and weighs 11 st 5 lb. He joined QPR at the end of 1972–3 season. Before that, as captain and centre-half of Arsenal, he won the 1970–71 League and Cup medals. Between May 3rd and May 8th, 1971 this was his amazing record: the League championship medal; selection for Scotland; elected 'Footballer of the Year' and finally he was a member of the triumphant Arsenal team that won the FA Cup.

BOB McNAB—Arsenal
Bob is Huddersfield born (July 20th, 1943), 11 st and 5 ft 9 in. In October 1966 Huddersfield Town transferred their former junior and reserve player —by this time a formidable full-back—to Arsenal for the record fee (at that time) of £50,000.

He was in Mexico with the England side for the World Cup but not given a place in the final 22.

However he was among the ITV experts who commented on the Finals for the British audience.

By the time Bob was made Arsenal captain in 1973 he had won four England caps (the first was in the match v. Rumania in November, 1968). He also won a Fairs Cup winners' medal in 1969–70 and League and FA Cup winners' medals, 1970–71.

BILLY McNEILL—Celtic

As captain and a distinguished centre-half, Billy is largely responsible for the dominating position of Celtic in Scottish football.

Winner of many medals, both Cup and Championship, one of his greatest triumphs was the gaining of a European Cup Winners' medal in 1967, playing against Inter-Milan in Lisbon.

BERTIE MEE—Arsenal Manager

Manager since March 1967, Bertie has brought the Highbury side some outstanding successes: League Championship, victory in the FA Cup Final and Fairs Cup Final and two League Cup Final appearances. Perhaps the highest point of Arsenal's comeback was in 1970–71 when they became the fourth team in football history to win the 'double' —the League and FA Cups.

IAN MELLOR—Norwich City

Former postman turned professional, Ian who is 6 ft 1 in tall and weighs in at 10 st 12 lb, is a native of Manchester. He had a keen following of fans in his Manchester City days at Maine Road.

His first League match was on March 20th, 1971 against Coventry City, and by the end of the 1970–71 season he had made six League appearances. The following season saw him firmly established at No. 11.

On March 7th, 1973 he transferred to Norwich for a £65,000 fee.

Which player

has a European Cup Winners' medal?
was once a postman?
is Irish?
scored in his first two matches as a first team player?

What do Bob McNab and Bertie Mee have in common?
What do Frank McLintock and Bob McNab have in common?
Who transferred from Manchester City to Norwich?

How many of the players have played for their respective countries?
Name them.
Which is the tallest of the players mentioned?
Which one is NOT a player?

What does QPR stand for?
Who was elected "Footballer of the Year"?

Who is your favourite sportsman?

Write a brief entry for him as it might appear in a *Who's Who of Sport*.

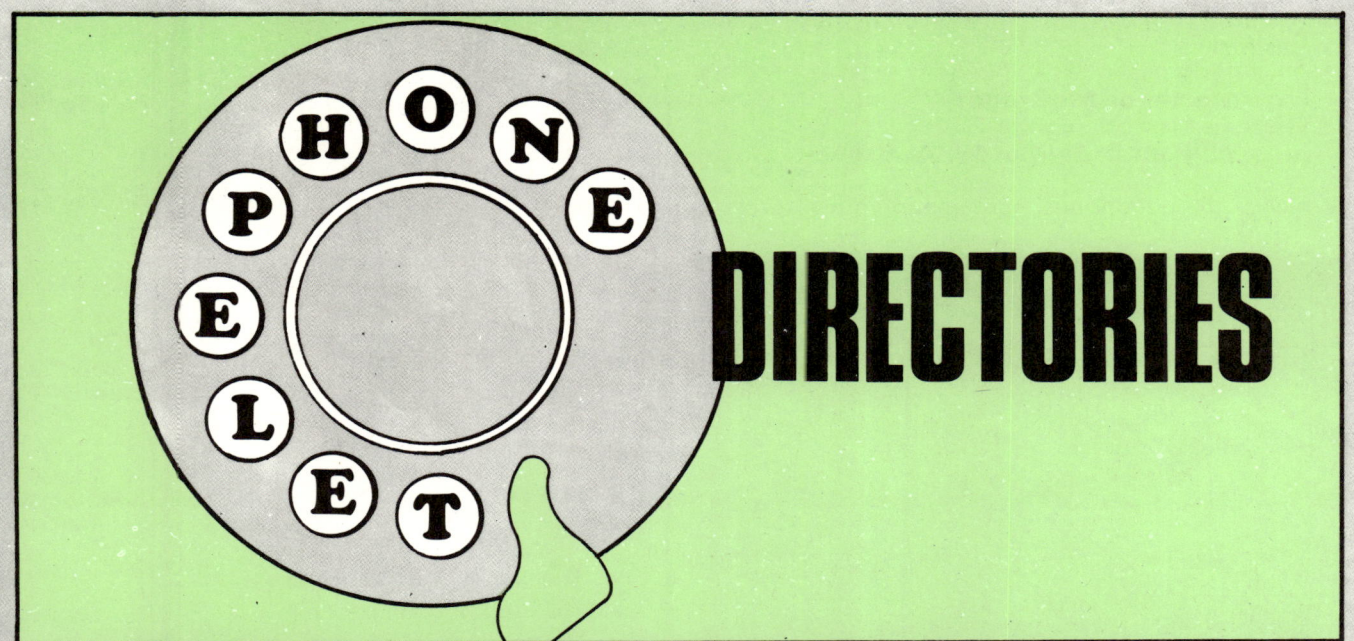

PHONE **DIRECTORIES**

This is part of a telephone directory.

```
Dewsford J, The Limes, Westport..........................186 2384
Dexter W.F, Frmr, Moorbank, Glenville....................282 3167
Deyne Sq.Ldr R, DFC, Westview, Westport..................186 9328
East S, Leather Goods, 21 Main St..................Langton 214
Easton Mrs W.N, Linden Lea, Lesburn......................364 1412
Eston News, Press Buildings, Eston
        Editor.............................................104 9623
        Advertisements....................................104 8296
Eston Park Golf Club, Eston Rd, Eston....................104 2493
Ettleforth Dr J, Surgery, Elm Rd, Longton................176 3214
        Residence 4 Hill St, Longton......................176 1486
Ettson Rev J, The Vicarage........................Coston 217
```

A telephone directory lists the names of people in alphabetical order.

As well as their names it gives their addresses and telephone number. Occasionally it also gives their occupations.

Write down the phone numbers of:

> Sam East, the saddler
> Eston Park Golf Club
> The editor of the *Eston News*
> Bill Dexter

What number would you ring

if you wished to invite Dr Ettleforth to a party?
if you wished to call him in to see a sick relative?
if you wished to place an advertisement in the *Eston News*?

People in the telephone directory are known as subscribers.

Which subscriber in our directory is: **a farmer?**
a woman? a clergyman? a serviceman?

Which town would you get if you phoned the following numbers?

104   186   176   364

Your Own Directory

From your own directory find the telephone number of:

> **your school**
> **your doctor**
> **your nearest railway station**
> **the editor of your local newspaper**
> **your nearest hospital**
> **any local shop**
> **a garage**
> **your nearest airport**

Check from your own directory which of these names comes first:

Martin or McGregor

William Brown or W. A. Brown

Which is the commonest surname in your district?

Almost every country in the world devotes sections of its telephone directories to business firms. Sometimes this business section is tacked on at the end of the normal directory. Sometimes the business section is printed in a separate volume.

Occasionally these business pages are printed in a different colour. In Britain, for instance, they are yellow, and the business section is known as the *Yellow Pages*.

JOINERS AND CARPENTERS (CONT'D)
Wilson T & Sons, Cornwall St.................................**156** 2251
Wright E, 2 High St.................................**Polville** 1345

KEYS—CUTTING
Express Key Co., Weir Rd.................................**156** 2174
Mason L., 4 Broombank Rd.................................**129** 3162

KITCHEN FURNITURE MANUFACTURERS
Pinewood Products Ltd., Annwood Industrial Estate... **242** 5673

KNITTING MACHINES—MANUFACTURERS AND SUPPLIERS
Nitmate, 4 Rockhill Rd.................................**Rockhill** 2348
Thomson J, Hill St.................................**Polville** 1472

KNITWEAR RETAILERS
Balta, 299 Bell Rd.................................**242** 4724
Barr, 4 Barnhead.................................**Langton** 163
Young A, Lesburn Ave.................................**146** 2442

LABEL MANUFACTURERS—SELF-ADHESIVE
Speedway Label Co., Annwood Industrial Estate.........**242** 5431

LABEL PRINTERS
A & A, Castle St.................................**Langton** 423
Smith W, 14 Hall Rd.................................**216** 3489

LADDER HIRERS
Smith & Jones Ltd., 144 London Rd.................................**Colston** 364

LADIES WEAR—HIRE SPECIALISTS
Bridal Wear, 28 High St.................................**Polville** 1764

LADIES WEAR—RETAIL
Adair, 221 Annwood Rd.................................**242** 5036
Dunmore K, 4 Benn Ave.................................**132** 6421

Here is an extract from a typical business section of a telephone directory.

If you wished to hire a ladder to do a special job, which firm would you contact?

Give the address of a carpenter in Polville.

If you wished to hire a wedding gown, which number would you ring?

Give a phone number you could ring if you wished to buy a dress.

Name a firm from which you could buy a knitted sweater.

How to find your way in the BIBLE

The Bible is a collection of books which tells us how God revealed Himself to man, first in the Jewish religion and later in the Christian faith.

It is divided into two sections—the Old Testament tells the story of events before Christ was born and the New Testament describes what happened from the birth of Christ onwards.

Here are the books of the Bible (Authorised Version):

Old Testament

Genesis	2 Chronicles	Daniel
Exodus	Ezra	Hosea
Leviticus	Nehemiah	Joel
Numbers	Esther	Amos
Deuteronomy	Job	Obadiah
Joshua	Psalms	Jonah
Judges	Proverbs	Micah
Ruth	Ecclesiastes	Nahum
1 Samuel	Song of Solomon	Habakkuk
2 Samuel	Isaiah	Zephaniah
1 Kings	Jeremiah	Haggai
2 Kings	Lamentations	Zechariah
1 Chronicles	Ezekiel	Malachi

New Testament

Matthew	Ephesians	Hebrews
Mark	Philippians	James
Luke	Colossians	1 Peter
John	1 Thessalonians	2 Peter
Acts	2 Thessalonians	1 John
Romans	1 Timothy	2 John
1 Corinthians	2 Timothy	3 John
2 Corinthians	Titus	Jude
Galatians	Philemon	Revelation

Which is the first book of the New Testament?
Which is the last book in the Old Testament?
Name the first and last books of the Bible.

Copy out this list, then put either OT (Old Testament) or NT (New Testament) after each book.

Colossians

Isaiah

Daniel

Mark

Ezekiel

Hebrews

Galatians

Esther

The Old Testament contains

5 Books of Law   2 Books of Wisdom

10 Books of History   4 Books of Poetry

4 Books of Stories   14 Books of Prophecy

Find out which books come under these headings.

Bible References

The Bible, as we have already learned, is divided into books.

Each book is divided into chapters. If you look at Genesis you will find that it has 50 chapters.

Each chapter is also divided into verses. The first chapter of Genesis, for instance, has 31 verses.

If we wish to refer to any passage in the Bible it is therefore very simple. First we give the name of the book, then the number of the chapter and finally the number of the verse.

A Bible reference looks like this:

John 11:35

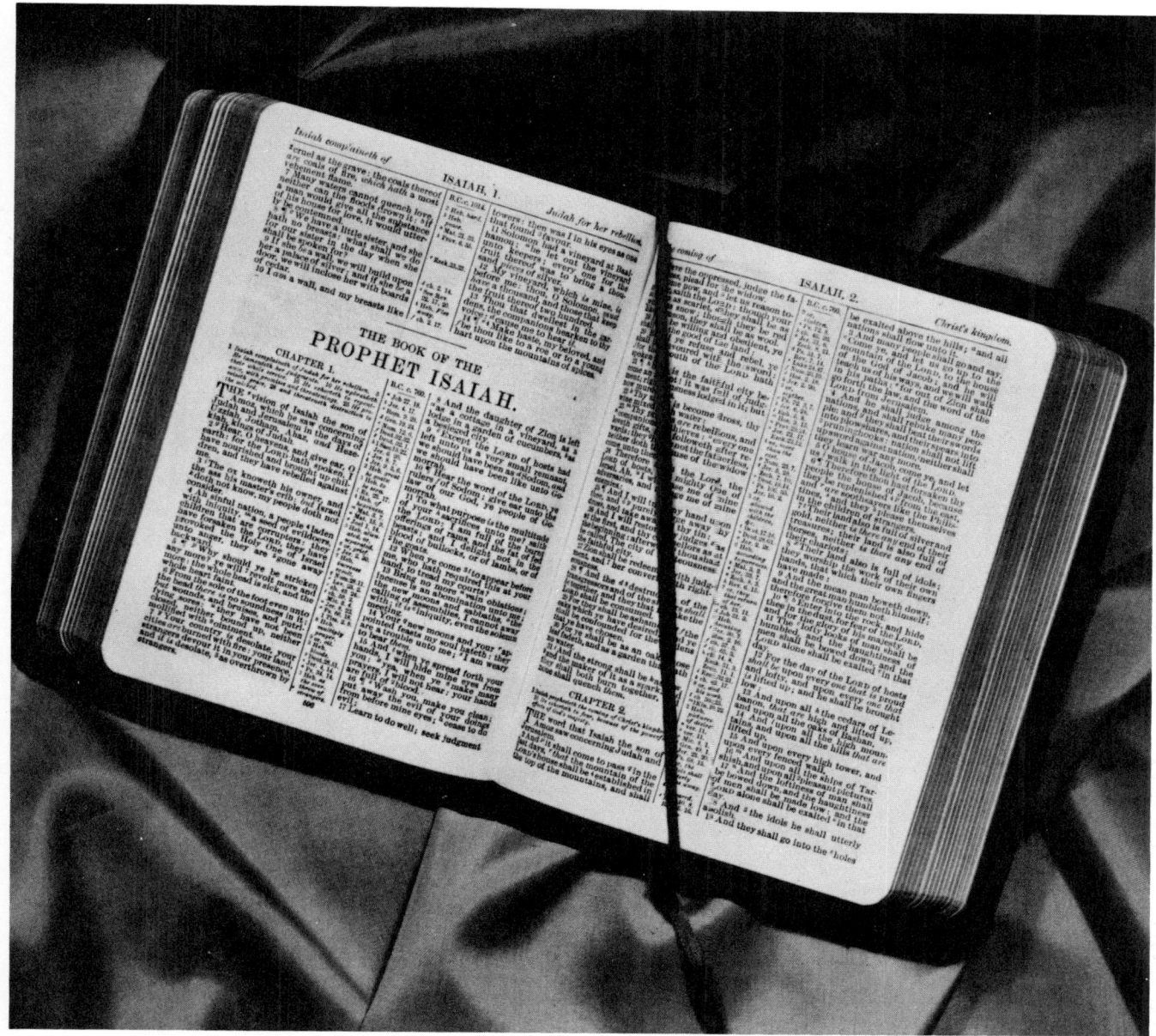

The book is Isaiah, the chapter is 2 and the verse is 4. Find out what the prophet says there about warring nations.

Which famous person in the Bible is mentioned in each of these passages?

Matthew	2:3	Genesis	28:16
Judges	15:16	Acts	16:28
Numbers	7:1	1 Kings	11:21
Mark	3:19	Daniel	3:2

How many different creatures are mentioned in Proverbs 30:25—31?

Which well-known story comes in Genesis 3? Write it out in your own words, in the way we speak nowadays. Then find a version of the Bible in modern English and compare the same story there with what you have written.

Sometimes it is difficult to find exactly what you are looking for in the Bible. Because it was written so long ago it has no index, of course. However, special Bible Dictionaries do exist to help you, and you can ask for them at your local library.

Here are the first and last words in one Bible Dictionary:

ACTS   **ZION**

What can you find out about them?

On this page you can see a picture of present-day Nazareth. Look up Matthew, 2:23. What was the name given to an inhabitant of Nazareth? See if you can find other mentions of Nazareth in the New Testament.

Identifying Things

Sometimes when you are out for a country walk you may see a particularly interesting bird or butterfly, but you may not know its name or anything about it. You can find out more from reference books which are specially written to help you to *identify* and to learn more about the animal, bird, fish, insect, flower, fossil, etc. which has attracted your attention.

Perhaps you like to go fishing, and if so you may be lucky enough to catch a fish known as a *roach*.

Here is a page with a drawing of a roach from a reference book about fishes.

You will notice that the fish is given a Latin name

"Rutilus rutilus".

Why do you think this is necessary?

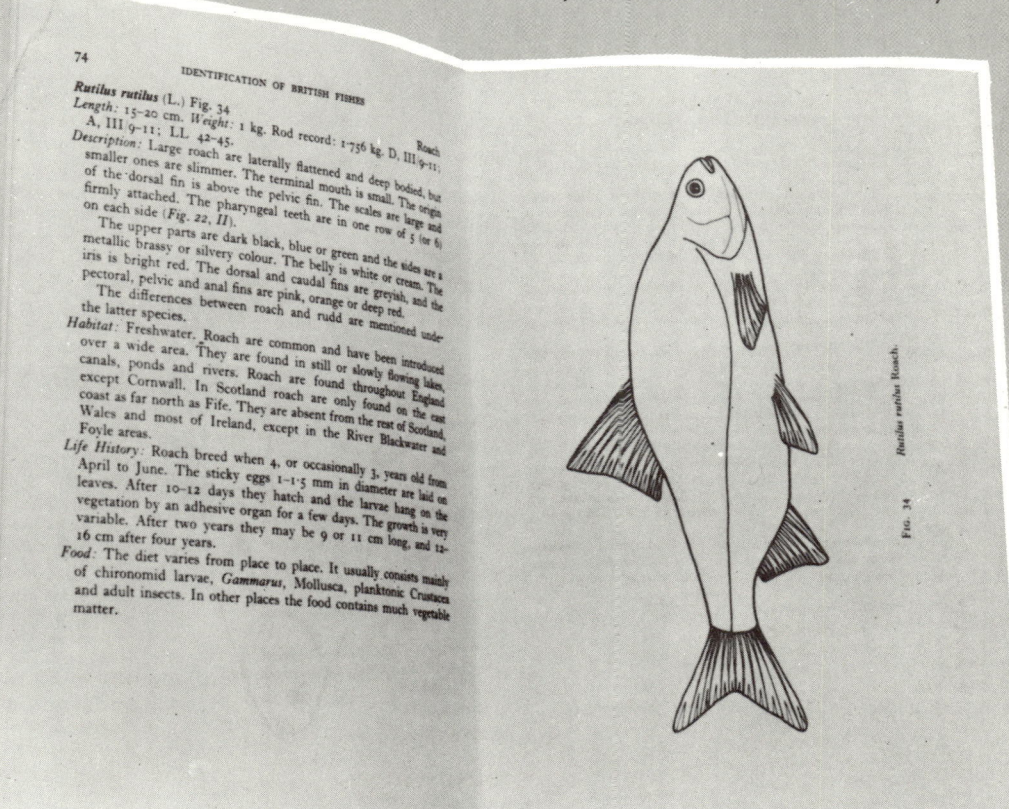

74   IDENTIFICATION OF BRITISH FISHES

Rutilus rutilus (L.) Fig. 34   Roach

Length: 15–20 cm. *Weight:* 1 kg. Rod record: 1·756 kg. D, III 9–11; A, III 9–11; LL 42–45.

Description: Large roach are laterally flattened and deep bodied, but smaller ones are slimmer. The terminal mouth is small. The origin of the dorsal fin is above the pelvic fin. The scales are large and firmly attached. The pharyngeal teeth are in one row of 5 (or 6) on each side (*Fig. 22, II*).

The upper parts are dark black, blue or green and the sides are a metallic brassy or silvery colour. The belly is white or cream. The iris is bright red. The dorsal and caudal fins are greyish, and the pectoral, pelvic and anal fins are pink, orange or deep red.

The differences between roach and rudd are mentioned under the latter species.

Habitat: Freshwater. Roach are common and have been introduced over a wide area. They are found in still or slowly flowing lakes, canals, ponds and rivers. Roach are found throughout England except Cornwall. In Scotland roach are only found on the east coast as far north as Fife. They are absent from the rest of Scotland, Wales and most of Ireland, except in the River Blackwater and Foyle areas.

Life History: Roach breed when 4, or occasionally 3, years old from April to June. The sticky eggs 1–1·5 mm in diameter are laid on leaves. After 10–12 days they hatch and the larvae hang on the vegetation by an adhesive organ for a few days. The growth is very variable. After two years they may be 9 or 11 cm long, and 12–16 cm after four years.

Food: The diet varies from place to place. It usually consists mainly of chironomid larvae, *Gammarus*, Mollusca, planktonic Crustacea and adult insects. In other places the food contains much vegetable matter.

Rutilus rutilus Roach.

Fig. 34

Some of the words used in this description of the roach may be difficult to understand, so make a point of looking them up in your dictionary:

laterally   pharyngeal   larvae

terminal   caudal   adhesive

dorsal   pectoral   chironomid

pelvic

What is the record catch for a roach?

What colour is the belly?

Where is the roach found?

How long do the eggs take to hatch?

What is the length of a fully grown roach?

Here are some interesting wild flowers.

Here are some different breeds of dog.

Get a book on wild flowers from the library and identify them.

Write down the names of as many as you can, then get a book from the library to identify those breeds you didn't know.

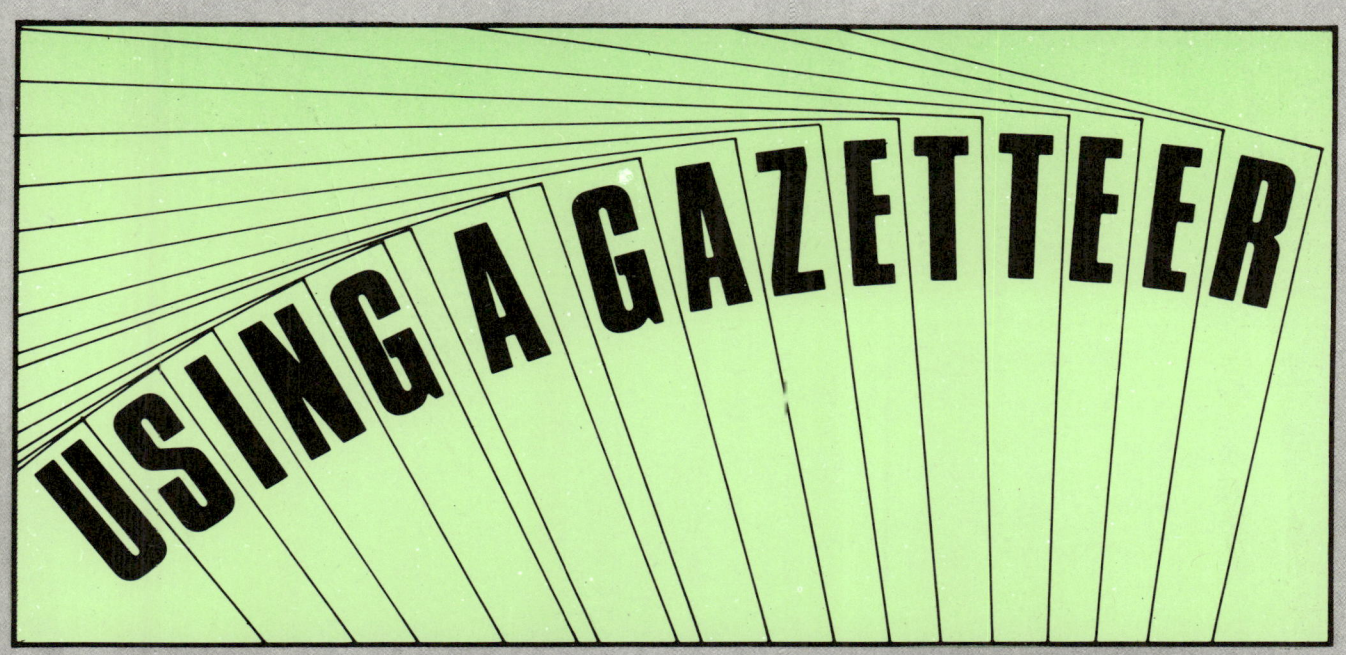

USING A GAZETTEER

A gazetteer is a reference book which lists place names in alphabetical order and gives brief details about them.

Below is a page from a gazetteer:

Medicine Hat Town and important railway junction in Alberta, Canada. It lies on the South Saskatchewan River and has a population of 25,000.

Medina A city of Saudi Arabia. It is second only to Mecca among the holy cities of the Moslem world. When Mohammed fled from Mecca it was to Medina he turned and his tomb is one of the most celebrated features of the city today. Population 50,000.

Medina A river of the Isle of Wight in Great Britain. It flows into the Solent at Cowes.

Mediterranean Sea The largest enclosed sea in the world. The Romans gave it its name (which means "Middle of the Earth" in Latin) because it was at the centre of the then known world. Its only natural connection with the open sea is the 15 km wide Strait of Gibraltar, but it also had a man-made connection with the Red Sea and the Indian Ocean by means of the Suez Canal.

Médoc A district in France famous for its wines. It lies on the left bank of the Gironde River.

Medway An English river which flows through Kent to the Thames estuary. Among the towns on its banks are Maidstone, Rochester and Chatham.

Megiddo An ancient city of Palestine (now Israel) on the plain of Esdraelon. In 609 B.C. Josiah was slain in battle here.

Mekong One of the great rivers of Asia. It rises in Tibet and flows southwards to the China Sea. For part of its course it forms the natural border between Laos and Siam (Thailand). Although its length is 4,500 km much of its course is impassable to shipping because of rapids.

Melbourne An Australian city at the mouth of the Yarra River. It is the chief city of Victoria and its many fine buildings include the university, the Houses of Parliament, the Law Courts, and two cathedrals. The city was named in 1837 after the Prime Minister, Lord Melbourne. Population 2,000,000.

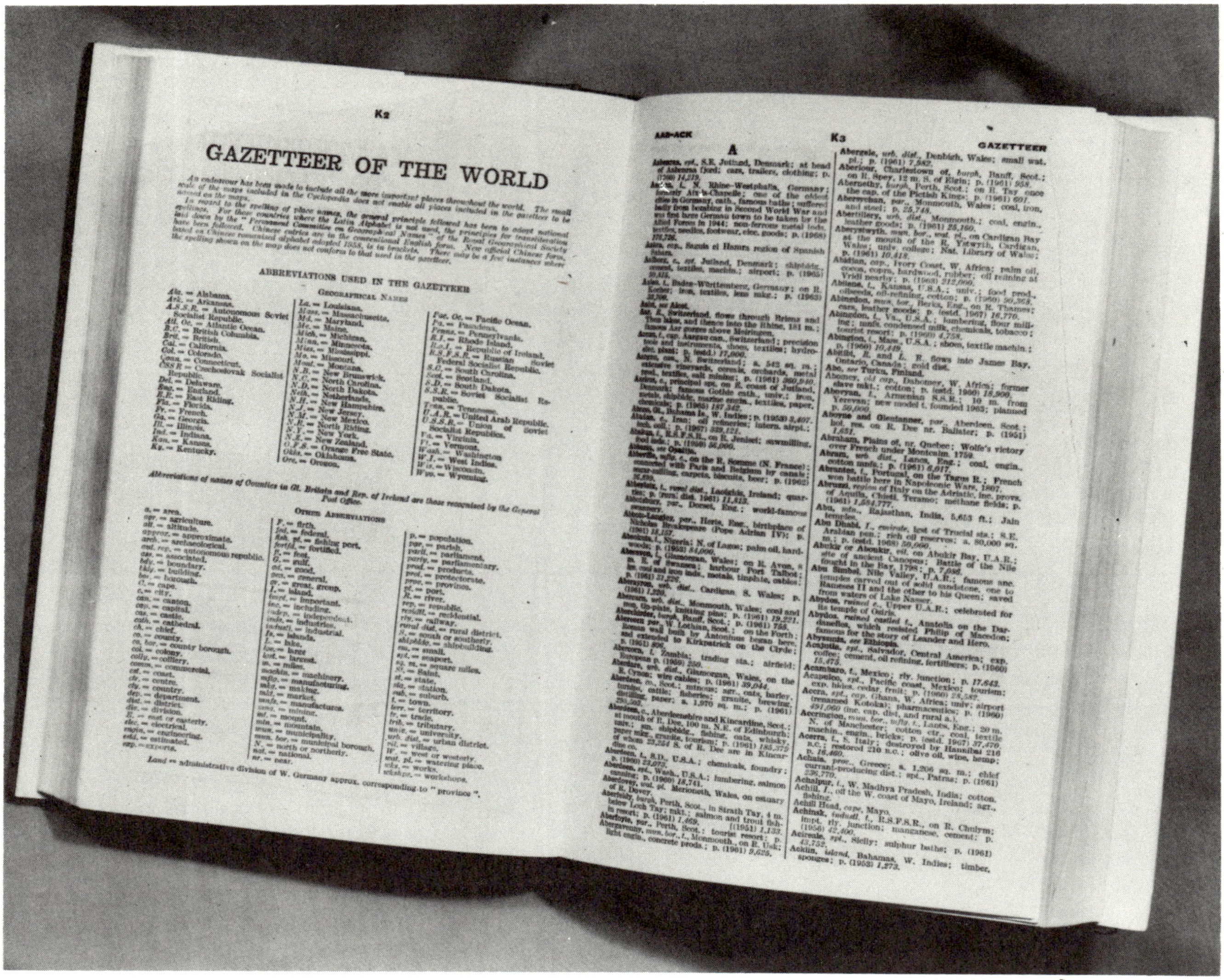

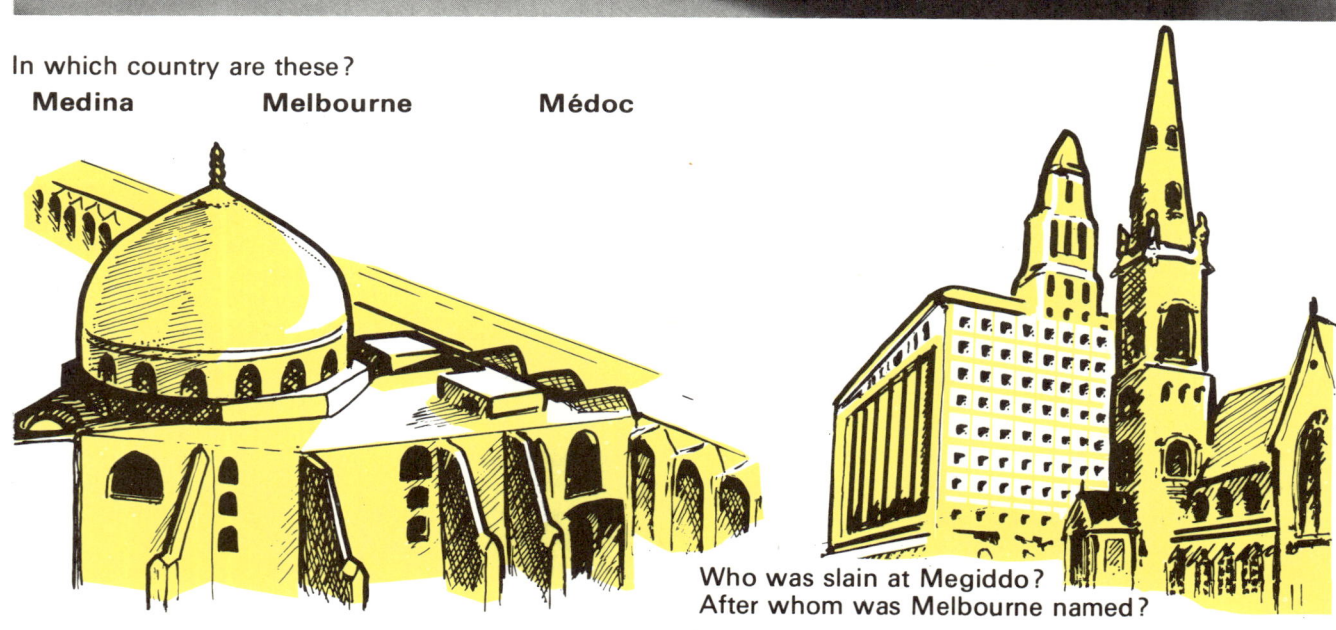

In which country are these?

Medina   **Melbourne**   **Médoc**

Who was slain at Megiddo?
After whom was Melbourne named?

The Aswan Dam on the River Nile

Megiddo—Remains of houses

Melbourne, Australia

For what is the district of Médoc famous?
Whose tomb is at Medina?

How did the Mediterranean Sea get its name?
Put these in order of population (the smallest first):
Medina, Medicine Hat, Melbourne.

The border between which two countries is formed by the Mekong River?
Which is the holiest city in the Moslem world?

How wide is the Strait of Gibraltar?
On which river does Maidstone stand?
Which town stands on the South Saskatchewan River?

How many of the following would you expect to find in a gazetteer?
Ecuador, canal, Napoleon Bonaparte, River Nile, estuary, Baffin Island.

Here are some place names.

Put them into alphabetical order, then, using what you know about them or can find out about them in any reference book, write a little gazetteer of your own for them.

Hudson Bay   **Hawaii**   **Holland**

Hebrides   **Huron**   **Hong Kong**

Hudson River   **Hastings**   **Hobart**

Hungary   **Humber**   **Havana**

Heidelberg   **Huddersfield**

MOTORIST'S HANDBOOK

As more and more motorists took to the road, books called motorist's handbooks were produced to help them with their journeys.

A motorist's handbook consists of a set of road maps followed by notes on the various places shown in the maps.

A page from a typical motorist's handbook looks something like this.

Barrtown Lanarkshire 4020 . . . .
Map 38C Lh 11.30–2.30 5–10
Edinburgh 47 Glasgow 32 London
372 Lanark 18 Barrtown Arms t.
124 5432 rm 6 ch P6 c ncp
BB £2: £3 M 60p: £1.20 W £22
Lm.

Bailford Glos. 1780   Map 24D
Lh 10–2.30 6–10.30
London 92 Cheltenham Spa 16
Chipping Norton 10 Oxford 30
Stratford 19 Warwick 24
Star Inn, High St, t. 221 1721 rm 18
pb 5 c tv ncp BB £2.50: £4 M
£1.50: £2.50 W £30: £35·Lm.

Swan, Warwick Rd, t. 221 1436
rm 15 pb 3 G pl4 c tv BB £2.50:
£3 M 75p: £1.50 W £25.

Bridham, Lancs. 68,140 Map 20B
Lh 11–3 5.30–10.30
London 187 Blackburn 36 Bolton 20
Chester 23 Liverpool 19 Manchester
17 Preston 31 Stoke-on-Trent 40
Wigan 14
Coach House, London Rd. t. 43921
rm 22 r G P 20 c tv ndg BB £3: £4
M £1.50: £2.50 Lm.
Commercial, Ashington St, t. 39624
rm 19 ch Np G P 15 c tv ncp
closed Dec 24–Dec 27 BB £2.50:
£3 M £1: £1.50.

Note: The prices given above are only examples and may not be the same as today's rates.

Which is the largest of the three towns?

Which one is in Scotland?

Which one is nearest to London?

Which one has the smallest population?

What do the following mean?
ncp   t   pb   ch   Lh *(Page 59 will help you).*

How many bedrooms are there in the Barrtown Arms?

Are coach parties allowed at the Star Inn?

What is the best hotel in Bridham?

Are children welcome at the Commercial?

Can you get a late meal at the Swan?

Which is the only hotel which does not provide its guests with television?

Which are the only two hotels with central heating throughout?

Name the hotels which do not list their weekly terms.

What is the lowest price you can pay for bed and breakfast at any of the hotels listed?

What is the highest price you can pay for a main meal?

Abbreviations

As you can see, a great many abbreviations are used in motorists' handbooks. Here is a list of the more common ones.

BB Bed and breakfast

c Children welcomed

ch Central heating throughout

G Garage accommodation

Lh Licensing hours

Lm Late meals

M Main meal

ncp No coach parties

Np Night porter

P Free parking (e.g. P6 means free parking for 6 vehicles)

pb Private bathrooms

r Radio in every bedroom

rm Bedrooms

t Telephone number

W Weekly terms

Rating (the more stars a hotel has, the better it is).

Using your own motorist's handbook find out the following facts:

Which is the largest hotel in your town or village?

What is its telephone number?

How many bedrooms are there?

Does it have garage accommodation?

Are coach parties welcome?

Do they supply late meals?

How much do they charge for bed and breakfast?

DOMI MINA
NUS· TIO·
ILLU MEA

Dictionaries of Quotations

Who Said What?

Famous quotations—well-known lines of poetry, from Shakespeare to limericks, popular sayings, nursery rhymes, songs, the memorable words of statesmen, generals, novelists and humorists—all these can be found in a dictionary of quotations.

Here are a few examples from *The Oxford Dictionary of Quotations*.

CECIL FRANCES ALEXANDER
1818–1895

20 Once in royal David's city
   Stood a lowly cattle shed,
Where a Mother laid her Baby
   In a manger for His bed:
Mary was that Mother mild
Jesus Christ her little Child.

Once in Royal David's City (1848)

RALPH HODGSON
1871–1962

5 'Twould ring the bells of Heaven
   The wildest peal for years,
If Parson lost his senses
   And people came to theirs,
And he and they together
   Knelt down with angry prayers
For tamed and shabby tigers
   And dancing dogs and bears,
And wretched, blind, pit ponies,
   And little hunted hares.

Poems. The Bells of Heaven

HENRY CHARLES BEECHING
1859–1919

3 With lifted feet, hands still,
I am poised, and down the hill
Dart, with heedful mind;
The air goes by in a wind.

Going Down Hill on a Bicycle

ALAN ALEXANDER MILNE
1882–1956

14 They're changing guard at Buckingham Palace—
Christopher Robin went down with Alice.

When We Were Very Young. Buckingham Palace

15 James James
Morrison Morrison
Weatherby George Dupree
Took great
Care of his Mother
Though he was only three.

Ib. Disobedience

17 The King asked
The Queen, and
The Queen asked
The Dairymaid:
'Could we have some butter for
The Royal slice of bread?'

Ib. The King's Breakfast

HORATIO, VISCOUNT NELSON
1758–1805

13 Palmam qui meruit, ferat.
   Let him who merits bear the palm.

Motto

14 Sent Admiral Collingwood the Nelson touch.

Private Diary, 9 Oct. 1805

23 England expects that every man will do his duty.

At the battle of Trafalgar. Ib.

24 This is too warm work, Hardy, to last long.

Ib.

25 Thank God, I have done my duty.

Ib.

26 Kiss me, Hardy.

Ib.

JOHN KEATS
1795–1821

10 Season of mists and mellow fruitfulness,
Close bosom-friend of the maturing sun;
Conspiring with him how to load and bless
With fruit the vines that round the thatch-eaves run.

To Autumn

Look at the quotations on page 60 and answer these questions:

In which poem by A. A. Milne do these lines occur?
'Could we have some butter for
The Royal slice of bread?'

Who wrote a poem called 'The Bells of Heaven'? What animals does the poem mention in the verse that is quoted? What does the poet feel about these animals?

Who was the author of 'Once in Royal David's City'? Give the dates when the author lived.

What is the title of a poem that begins 'With lifted feet, hands still'?

Let us say you have only a vague memory of a quotation and wish to check its exact wording. How will you find it in the dictionary of quotations?

If you know the author's name your task is simple. *The Oxford Dictionary of Quotations* sets out its authors in alphabetical order, beginning with Peter Abelard and ending with Emile Zola. Other dictionaries may provide a separate alphabetical index.

But if you do not know who the author is you will have to consult the Index. It runs into many pages and it is a good idea to practise using it.

Look at the chart on the right hand side of this page. It tells you how to use a dictionary of quotations to track down the particular saying you want. It tells you who wrote these words and the book or poem in which they occur.

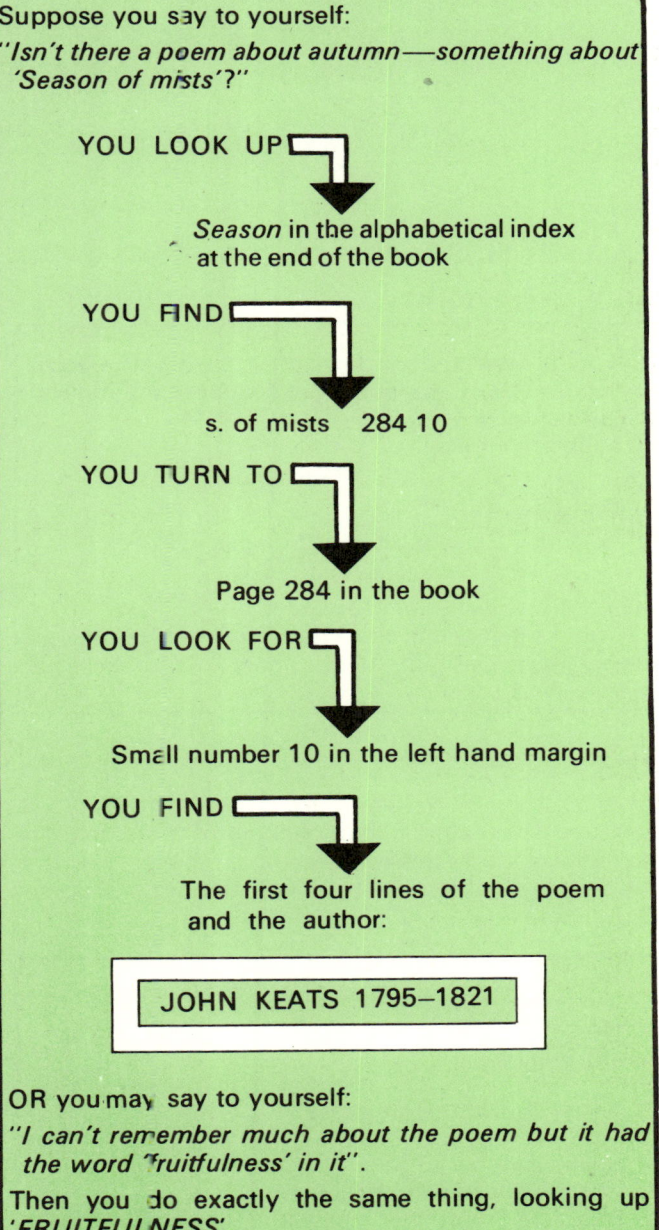

Suppose you say to yourself:
"Isn't there a poem about autumn—something about 'Season of mists'?"

YOU LOOK UP

Season in the alphabetical index at the end of the book

YOU FIND

s. of mists   284 10

YOU TURN TO

Page 284 in the book

YOU LOOK FOR

Small number 10 in the left hand margin

YOU FIND

The first four lines of the poem and the author:

JOHN KEATS 1795–1821

OR you may say to yourself:
"I can't remember much about the poem but it had the word 'fruitfulness' in it".

Then you do exactly the same thing, looking up *'FRUITFULNESS'*.

This is what the Index looks like. It lists subjects by their first letter.

Below are some lines from poems. Try to discover how each verse goes on and give the author's name.

Find a well-known Christmas carol by Cecil Frances Alexander in the extracts from the Index shown on this page.

Find a line from 'Going Down Hill on a Bicycle' in the Index. (Use a word beginning with H.)

Find a reference to the Ralph Hodgson poem in the Index, using the word 'tigers'.

'There was an Old Man with a beard,
Who said, 'It is just as I feared!—'
(find three more lines)

'Nicholas Nye was lean and grey,
Lame of a leg and old,
More than a score of donkey's years
He had seen since he was foaled.'
(find four more lines)

Now see if you can use a dictionary of quotations to find where the following lines come from. Give the name of the author and the title of the book or poem each time.

'Do you believe in fairies?... If you believe, clap your hands!'

'Speak roughly to your little boy,
And beat him when he sneezes.'

Give the names and dates of the authors who wrote these lines:

'The Camel's hump is an ugly lump
Which well you may see at the Zoo.

'Fifteen men on the dead man's chest
Yo-ho-ho, and a bottle of rum!'

Atlases and Maps

An atlas is a book of maps. Do you know how it came to have that name? Try looking it up in an encyclopaedia.

Before you use an atlas it is essential to understand a little about maps.

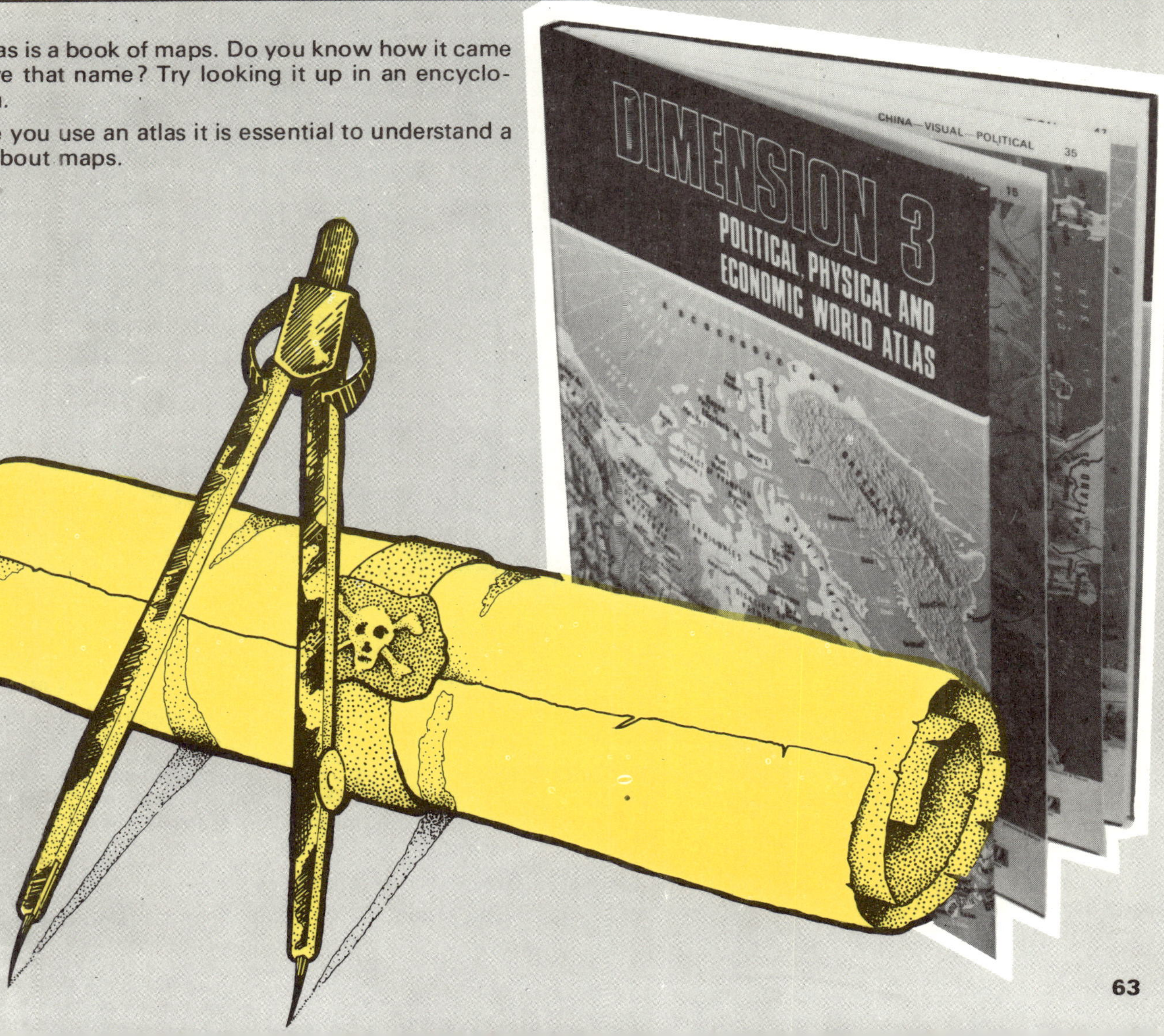

DIMENSION 3
POLITICAL, PHYSICAL AND
ECONOMIC WORLD ATLAS

CHINA—VISUAL—POLITICAL

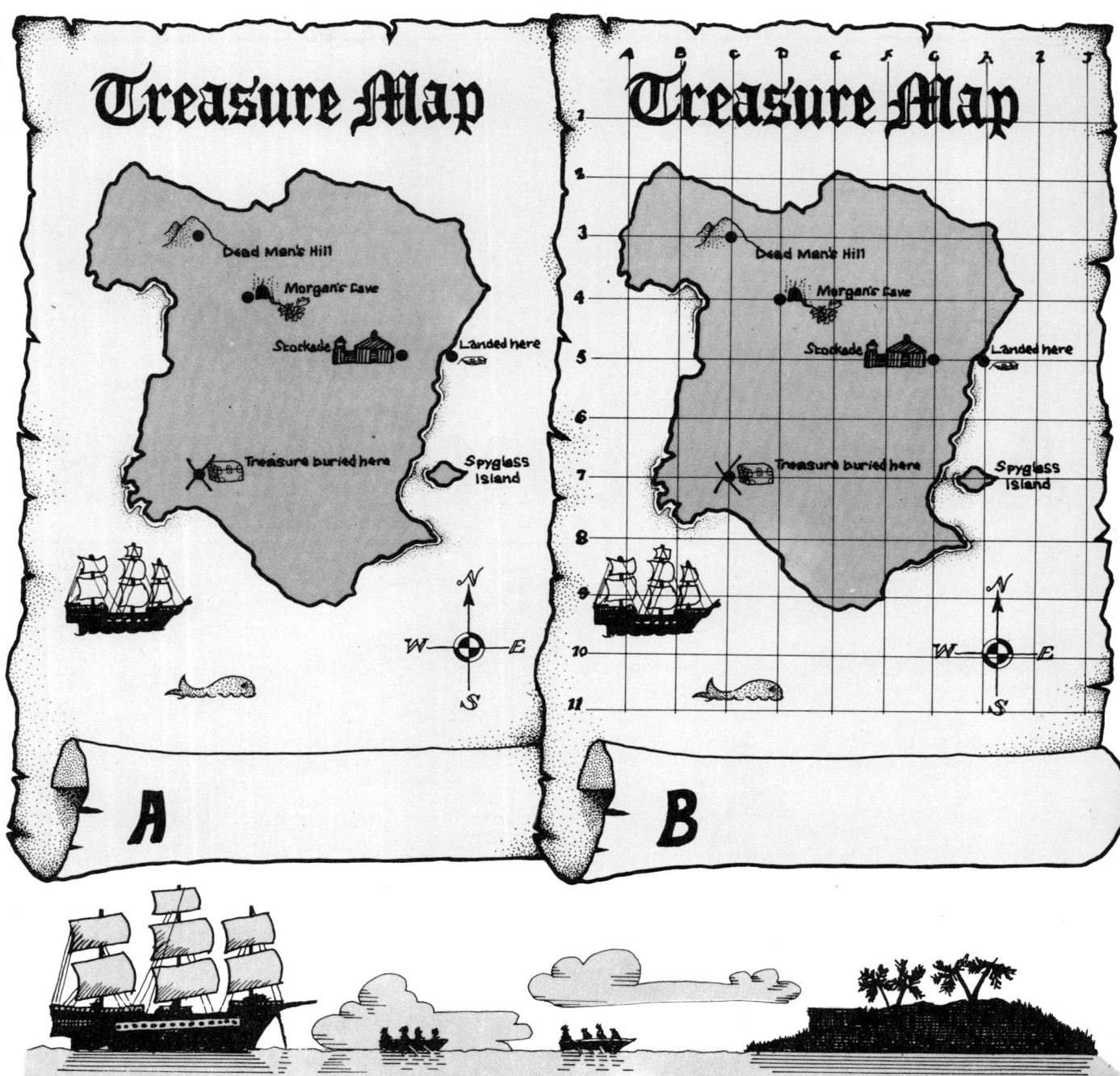

Marking a Position

On the pirate's treasure map A 'X' marks the spot where the treasure is buried.

From a map such as this it would be difficult to tell anyone exactly where to start digging.

We should have to give some vague directions like "south of Morgan's Cave" or "west of Spyglass Island."

Grid System

It was in order to give an exact map reference that the grid system was invented.

Map B shows a grid drawn over Treasure Island. We have lettered the north-to-south lines from A to J. We have numbered the west-to-east lines from 1 to 11.

We can now pinpoint any position on the map by giving first a letter and then a number.

Take the map reference D4. That means you go down the line marked D until you come to the point where it crosses the line marked 4. What would you find at this spot?

Give the map references for:

Dead Man's Hill; Spyglass Island; the buried treasure.

Latitude and Longitude

On ordinary maps the grid is slightly different. The equator is given the number 0. Lines are drawn at every 10° north and south of it. These are known as lines of latitude.

When it comes to the north-to-south lines, a line is drawn through Greenwich in England and is given the number 0. Lines are drawn at every 10° east and west of it. These are known as lines of longitude. An ordinary map would then look something like this.

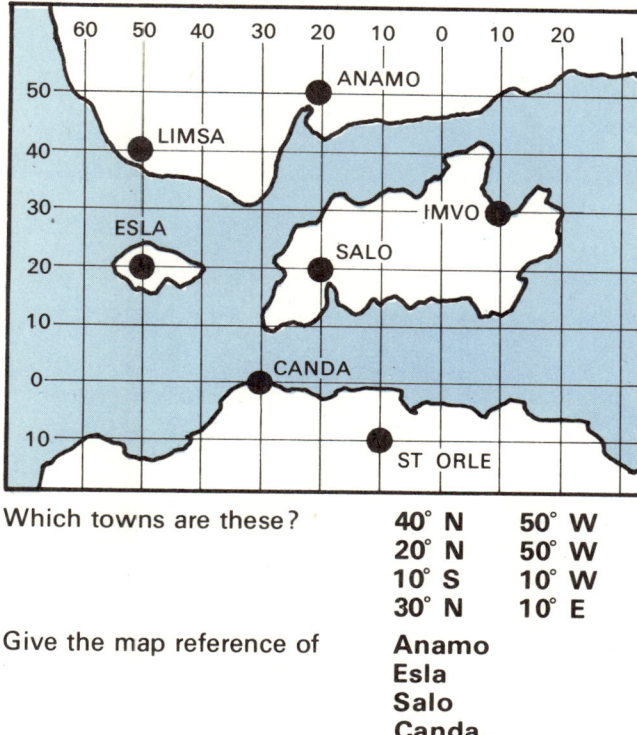

Which towns are these?

40° N   50° W
20° N   50° W
10° S   10° W
30° N   10° E

Give the map reference of   Anamo
Esla
Salo
Canda.

Here is a page taken from the index of a typical atlas.

Huddersfield	Engl.	$53\frac{1}{2}$N	$75\frac{1}{4}$E
Hudson r.	U.S.A.	42N	74W
Hudson str.	Can.	63N	70W
Hudson b.	Can.	60N	85W
Huelva	Spain	42N	0
Hughenden	Austr.	21S	144E
Hull	Can.	45N	76W
Hull	Engl.	$53\frac{3}{4}$N	$0\frac{3}{4}$W
Humansdorp	S. Afr.	34S	25E
Humber r.	Engl.	$53\frac{1}{2}$N	0
Humboldt	Can.	52N	105W
Hungerford	Engl.	$51\frac{1}{2}$N	$1\frac{1}{2}$W
Hu-nan pr.	China	27N	110E
Hunstanton	Engl.	53N	$0\frac{1}{2}$E
Huntingdon	Engl.	$52\frac{1}{4}$N	$0\frac{1}{4}$W
Huntly	Scot.	$57\frac{1}{2}$N	$2\frac{3}{4}$W
Huntsville	U.S.A.	35N	87W
Hu-peh pr	China	31N	112E
Huron l.	N. Amer.	44N	83W
Hurunui r.	N. Zeal.	$42\frac{3}{4}$S	$173\frac{1}{4}$E
Hwang Ho r.	China	35N	115E
Hyde	Engl.	$53\frac{1}{2}$N	2W
Hyderabad	India	26N	68E
Hythe	Engl.	51N	1E
Iceland i.	Eur.	65N	20W
Idaho st.	U.S.A.	44N	115W
Ilford	Engl.	$51\frac{1}{2}$N	0
Ilfracombe	Engl.	$51\frac{1}{4}$N	4W
Ilkley	Engl.	54N	$1\frac{3}{4}$W
Illimani mt.	Bolivia	17S	67W
Illinois st & r	U.S.A.	40N	90W
Ilmen l.	U.S.S.R.	58N	32E
Imbros i.	Turkey	40N	26E
Inchkeith i.	Scot.	56N	$3\frac{1}{4}$W
Indiana st	U.S.A.	40N	86W
Indianapolis	U.S.A.	40N	86W
Indus r.	India	29N	70E
Inn r.	Ger.	48N	12E

The Atlas and its Index

Like other reference books, the atlas has an alphabetical index—and very useful it is. It is not quite the same as the indexes you meet in other books, but easy to understand with a little practice.

Let us say you wish to find the town of Humboldt in your atlas. Your first problem is that you don't know which country to look up. Humboldt sounds slightly German. Could it be in Germany—or Switzerland—or is it just English enough to be in South Africa or the U.S.A.?

That is the first piece of information you get when you look Humboldt up in the index. It is in Canada, so it is to the map of Canada you must turn.

Canada, however, is a very big country. Do you look for Humboldt in the north, south, west or east?

The index now gives its exact map reference so that you can pinpoint it on the map.

Try these from the Index

In which country is each of these places?

Hyderabad   Inchkeith   Huntsville   Ilford

Are the following north or south of the equator?

**Idaho   Humansdorp   Hurunui   Imbros
Hughenden**

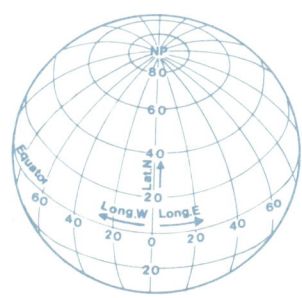

The globe illustrating Latitude and Longitude

In the index various abbreviations are used. What do these abbreviations stand for?

l   st   str   b   t   i

Here are some map positions.

Using your own atlas check up where each one is on the map. Write down the name of the country each one is in.

58N 40E	19N 99W	33S 14SE
48N 2E	27N 31E	32N 65W
	6N 7E	44S 173E

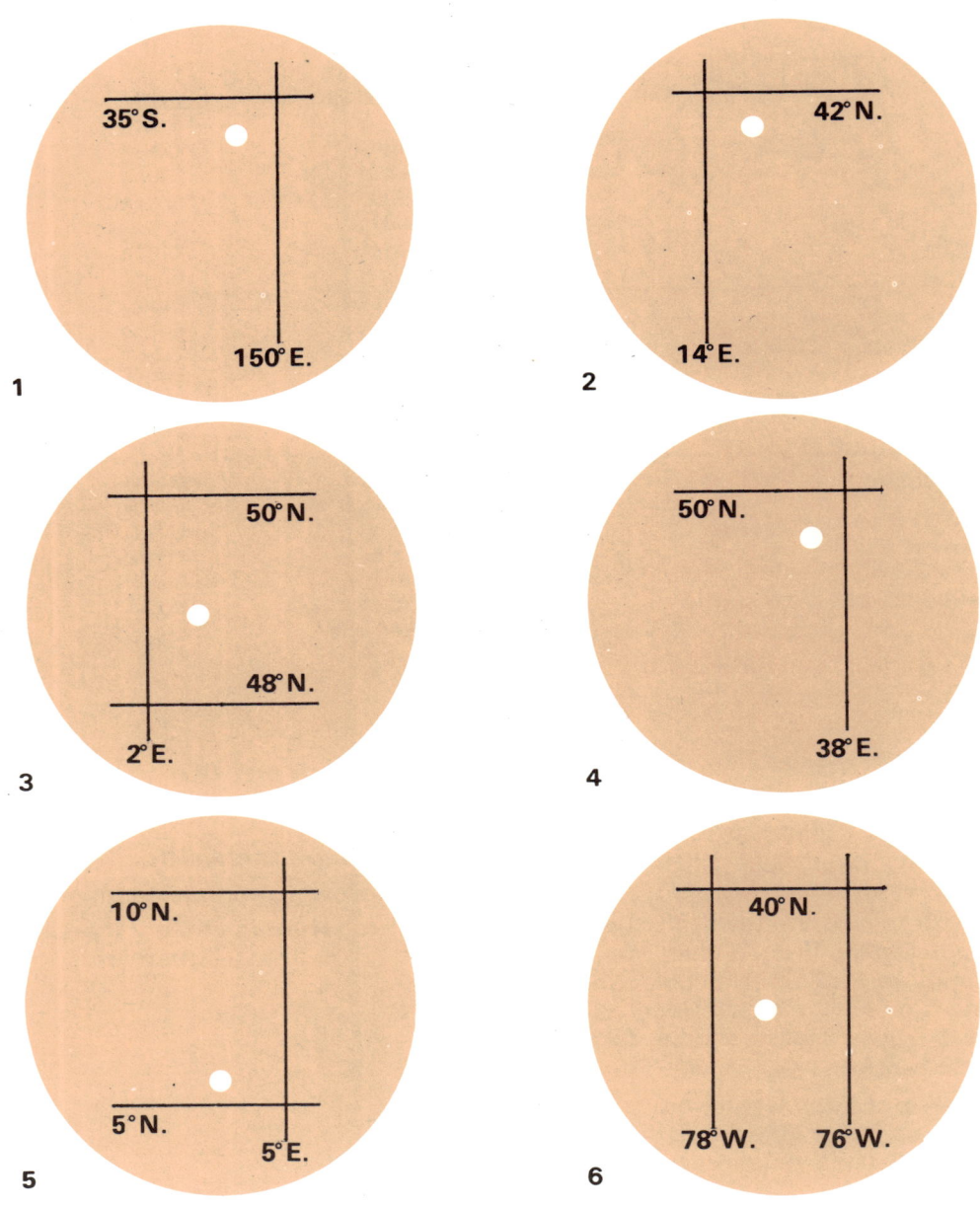

1

2

3

4

5

6

Here are six of the world's capital cities. Work out which they are and name the country in each case.

THE BOOK OF RECORDS

If you win the 100 metres race at your school sports the headmaster will probably be able to tell you whether or not you have broken the school record.

Most schools keep a note of these. They have the results dating right back to the first year the school sports were held, and they know who, in all that time, has run the fastest 200 metres, has jumped highest at the high jump, etc.

In much the same way world records are kept for sports all over the world. If you want to know a particular record in any sport you have to consult a book of records.

One of the best known books of records is the famous *Guinness Book of Records*. Many of the records in it are serious achievements. Others are unusual or amusing.

Facts About The Guinness Book of Records

It was started by twin brothers, Norris and Ross McWhirter.

The first book appeared in 1955.

It has now been reprinted 23 times.

There are now sixteen different editions printed in different parts of the world.

The book has been translated into the following languages:

French, Danish, German, Norwegian, Japanese, Spanish, Italian, Finnish, Swedish, Dutch, Czech, Portuguese, Hebrew and Serbo-Croatian.

Are you interested in pets? Then you might like to know some curious records that have been collected. Take cats, for instance. Here are some surprising facts about them. Did you know that the largest litter ever recorded was 13 kittens born to a blue pointed Siamese cat in Australia in 1969? Did you know that the Civil Service employs about 100,000 cats?

Now find out the names of two cats who were left a fortune in 1963. What was the home town of a cat that had 343 kittens? How many rats did the champion ratter kill? Who owned the greatest mouser on record?

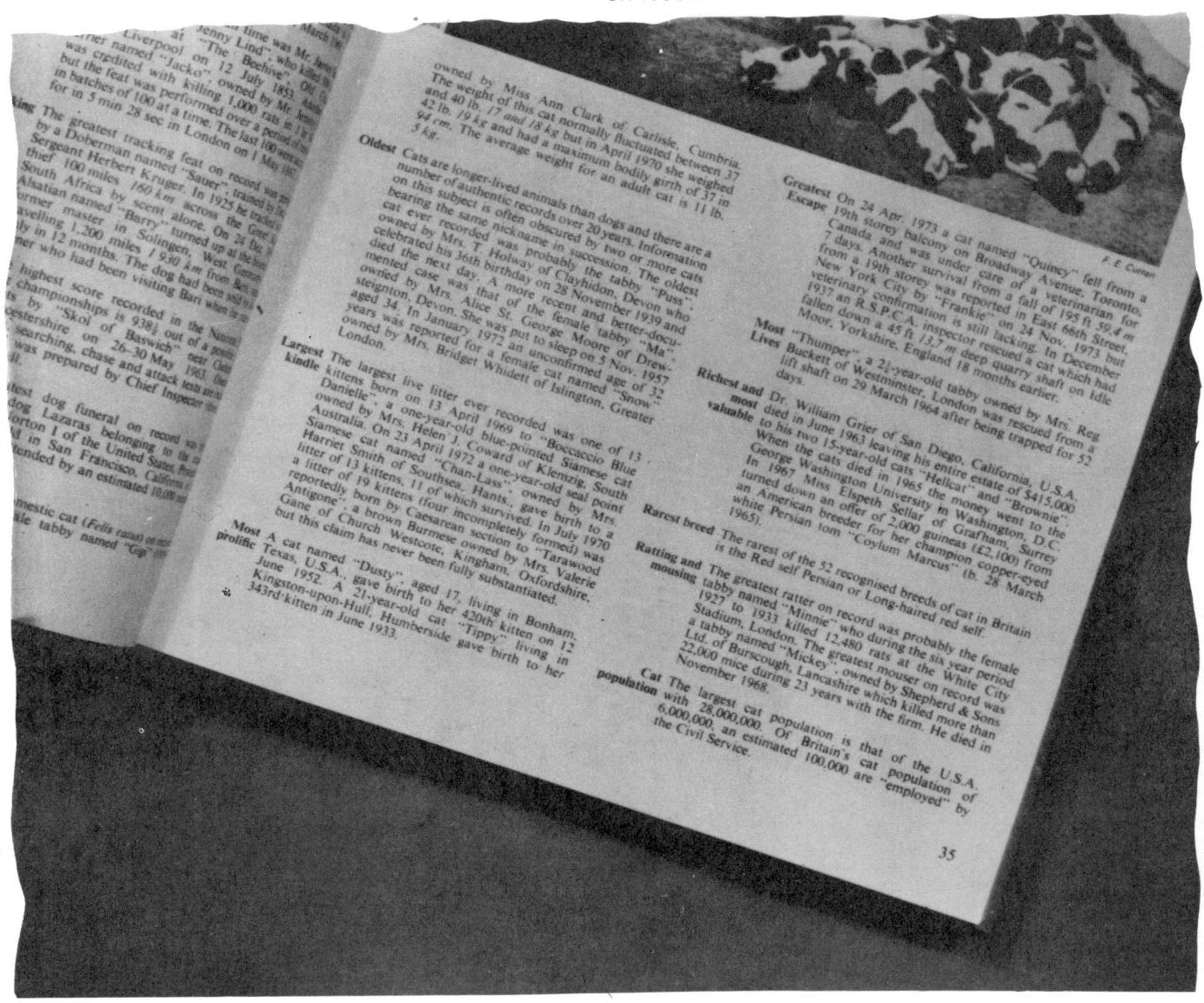

P. E. Curran

Oldest Cats are longer-lived animals than dogs and there are a number of authentic records over 20 years. Information on this subject is often obscured by two or more cats bearing the same nickname in succession. The oldest cat ever recorded was probably the tabby "Puss" owned by Mrs. T. Holway of Clayhidon, Devon who celebrated his 36th birthday on 28 November 1939 and died the next day. A more recent and better-documented case was that of the female tabby "Ma" owned by Mrs. Alice St. George Moore of Drewsteignton, Devon. She was put to sleep on 5 Nov. 1957 aged 34. In January 1972 an unconfirmed age of 32 years was reported for a female cat named "Snow" owned by Mrs. Bridget Whidett of Islington, Greater London.

Largest The largest live litter ever recorded was one of 13 **kindle** kittens born on 13 April 1969 to "Boccaccio Blue Danielle", a one-year-old blue-pointed Siamese cat owned by Mrs. Helen J. Coward of Klemzig, South Australia. On 23 April 1972 a one-year-old seal point Siamese cat named "Chan-Lass", owned by Mrs. Harriet Smith of Southsea, Hants., gave birth to a litter of 13 kittens, 11 of which survived. In July 1970 a litter of 19 kittens (four incompletely formed) was reportedly born by Caesarean section to "Tarawood Antigone", a brown Burmese owned by Mrs. Valerie Gane of Church Westcote, Kingham, Oxfordshire, but this claim has never been fully substantiated.

Most A cat named "Dusty", aged 17, living in Bonham, **prolific** Texas, U.S.A., gave birth to her 420th kitten on 12 June 1952. A 21-year-old cat "Tippy", living in Kingston-upon-Hull, Humberside gave birth to her 343rd kitten in June 1933.

owned by Miss Ann Clark of Carlisle, Cumbria. The weight of this cat normally fluctuated between 37 and 40 lb. *17 and 18 kg* but in April 1970 she weighed 42 lb. *19 kg* and had a maximum bodily girth of 37 in *94 cm*. The average weight for an adult cat is 11 lb. *5 kg*.

Greatest On 24 Apr. 1973 a cat named "Quincy" fell from a **Escape** 19th storey balcony on Broadway Avenue, Toronto, Canada and was under care of a veterinarian for 7 days. Another survival from a fall of 195 ft *59.4 m* from a 19th storey was reported in East 66th Street, New York City by "Frankie" on 24 Nov. 1973 but veterinary confirmation is still lacking. In December 1937 an R.S.P.C.A. inspector rescued a cat which had fallen down a 45 ft. *13.7 m* deep quarry shaft on Idle Moor, Yorkshire, England 18 months earlier.

Most "Thumper", a 2½-year-old tabby owned by Mrs. Reg **Lives** Buckett of Westminster, London was rescued from a lift shaft on 29 March 1964 after being trapped for 52 days.

Richest and Dr. William Grier of San Diego, California, U.S.A. **most** died in June 1963 leaving his entire estate of $415,000 **valuable** to his two 15-year-old cats "Hellcat" and "Brownie". When the cats died in 1965 the money went to the George Washington University in Washington, D.C. In 1967 Miss Elspeth Sellar of Grafham, Surrey turned down an offer of 2,000 guineas (£2,100) from an American breeder for her champion copper-eyed white Persian tom "Coylum Marcus" (b. 28 March 1965).

Rarest breed The rarest of the 52 recognised breeds of cat in Britain is the Red self Persian or Long-haired red self.

Ratting and The greatest ratter on record was probably the female **mousing** tabby named "Minnie" who during the six year period 1927 to 1933 killed 12,480 rats at the White City Stadium, London. The greatest mouser on record was a tabby named "Mickey", owned by Shepherd & Sons Ltd. of Burscough, Lancashire which killed more than 22,000 mice during 23 years with the firm. He died in November 1968.

Cat The largest cat population is that of the U.S.A. **population** with 28,000,000. Of Britain's cat population of 6,000,000, an estimated 100,000 are "employed" by the Civil Service.

35

Print order The print order for the 48th Automobile Association Members' Handbook (1974–75) was 5,300,000 copies. The total print since 1908 has been 64,010,000. It is currently printed by web offset by Petty & Sons of Leeds.

Largest cartoon The largest cartoon ever exhibited was one covering five storeys (50 × 150 ft [15 × 45 m]) of a University of Arizona building drawn by Dr. Peter A. Kesling for Mom 'n Dad's Day 1954.

Longest lived strip The most durable newspaper comic strip has been the Katzenjammer Kids (Hans and Fritz) created by Rudolph Dirks and first published in New York on 12 Dec. 1897 and currently drawn by Joe Musial. The earliest strip was Little Bear by Jim Lyons (b. 1876) which first appeared in the *San Francisco Examiner* in 1894.

LETTERS

Longest The longest personal letter based on a word count is one of 325,000 words by Anton van Dam of Arnheim, Netherlands to his pen pal Clementi between 24 June 1940 and 15 July 1945. Clementi however became Mrs. H. Randolph Holder.

To an editor **Longest** The longest recorded letter to an editor was one of 13,000 words (a third of a modern novel) written to the editor of the *Fishing Gazette* by A.R.I.E.L. and published in 7-point type spread over two issues in 1884.

Most Britain's, and seemingly the world's, most indefatigable writer of letters to the editors of newspapers is Raymond L. Cantwell, 52, of Oxford, who since 1948 has had more than 12,000 letters published in print or on the air. His peak production has been 425 in 36 hours non-stop in aid of charity.

Shortest The shortest correspondence on record was that between Victor Marie Hugo (1802–85) and his publisher Hurst and Blackett in 1862. The author was on holiday and anxious to know how his new novel *Les Misérables* was selling. He wrote "?". The reply was "!".

Victor Hugo (1802–1885), author, in 1862, of the shortest letter on record

This is part of a page from the *Guinness Book of Records* section on 'The Arts and Entertainment'.

Can you discover in which newspaper the earliest strip cartoon appeared and when?

What was the size of the largest cartoon ever exhibited? Who drew it?

What was the length of the longest recorded letter to an editor?

What is the name of the man in the photograph? Find out what his nationality was. Look him up in an encyclopaedia and see what you can discover about him.

Below you will see some more records of different kinds.

Riding in armour The longest recorded ride in full armour is one of 146 miles *234,9 km* from Glasgow to Dumfries *via* Lanark and Peebles, Scotland in 3 days 3 hrs 40 min by Dick Brown 42 on 12–15 June 1973.

Riveting The world's record for riveting is 11,209 in 9 hours by J. Moir at the Workman Clark Ltd. shipyard, Belfast, Northern Ireland, in June 1918. His peak hour was his seventh with 1,409, an average of nearly 23½ per min.

Rocking-chair The longest recorded duration of a "Rockathon" is 307 hrs 30 min by Michael Smith of Aubrey, California, U.S.A., at the Fresno Fashion Fair on 24 Aug. –6 Sept. 1972.

Rolling pin The record distance for a woman to throw a 2 lb. *907 g* rolling pin is 144 ft 4 in *43,89 m* by Sherri Salyer at Stroud, Oklahoma on 18 July 1970.

What was Sherri Salyer's record-breaking feat in July 1970?

What was Dick Brown's strange method of travelling in Scotland in June 1973?

Name the shipyard where J. Moir broke the riveting record in 1918?

In which year and where did the longest 'Rockathon' take place?

Unusual Records

Do you think there are still records left you could break? Perhaps some unusual little-known record is just waiting for a new champion to come along?

Do you feel, for instance, you could peel an apple and produce a longer unbroken peel than anyone else? Or demolish a piano at record speed? Could you set a record for skipping? Or even speak for longer than anyone else?

The *Guinness Book of Records* covers these unusual records too. Check your chances against the world record holders listed on the next page.

Crazy Records

Frank Freer (U.S.A.) produced an unbroken apple peel of 130 ft 8½ ins (39 m 86 cm) in 1971. The record time for demolishing an upright piano is 2 minutes 26 seconds, set by a team from Ireland in 1968. The greatest number of turns in skipping is 32,089 by J. P. Hughes of Melbourne, Australia in 3 hours 10 minutes in 1953. The world record for non-stop talking is 138 hours (5 days 18 hours), set by Victor Villimas of Cleveland, U.S.A. in 1967.

Using the index, find out to which page you would have to turn to obtain details of the following:

The longest serving Member of Parliament
The fastest pancake race
The earliest number plate
The lowest night club
The deepest crater on the moon
The largest octopus
The dullest set of matchbox labels
The tallest maypole.

DAILY WEATHER

Some of the facts we need are not permanent enough to be in the form of books. Topical information, that is information which changes all the time, is published in newspapers.

A newspaper's job is to give its readers the daily news. It tells them about important events at home and abroad, and many items of general interest such as football results, reviews of new films and stage shows, radio and television programmes and the *weather*.

World Weather

One part of the weather news describes what sort of weather people were enjoying (or suffering) at different places in the world at noón yesterday. Many newspapers use the same simple code:

c—cloudy; f—fair; r—rain; s—sunny

The temperature at each place is also given, usually on the Centigrade and Fahrenheit scales. A newspaper description of world weather looks something like this (this is only part of the list):

Which city had rain at noon yesterday?
Which city in *north-west Europe* was sunny?
Which was the hottest city at noon yesterday?
What was the highest temperature recorded?
Name the warmest *European* city.
Which was the coolest city at noon yesterday?
Three of the cities are in the British Isles: which was the warmest?

British newspapers give more weather space to the British Isles than to the rest of the world. Some, for example, name the warmest, coldest, sunniest and wettest places on the previous day, and the times that the sun and moon rise and set. Some have a picture showing the shape of the moon:

This is called a *gibbous moon*—between half moon and full moon or vice versa.

Some newspapers list the number of sunshine hours at various coastal towns, including holiday resorts, yesterday. The next page gives an example.

World Weather—Noon Yesterday

		C	F				C	F
Algiers	c	19	66		Berlin	c	13	55
Amsterdam	s	13	55		Biarritz	f	12	54
Athens	s	22	72		Birmingham	c	11	52
Barcelona	s	16	61		Bombay	f	35	95
Beirut	s	25	77		Bristol	c	10	50
Belfast	r	5	41		Brussels	f	13	55

A seaside resort which has become world famous largely because of its long hours of sunshine in all seasons of the year: Nice, on the French Riviera, with its beach stretching round the Baie des Anges and the parallel Promenade des Anglais (right).

Sunshine Hours—24 Hours to 7 p.m.

Hours of Sunshine

Aberdeen	6.2	Jersey	13.4
Aberystwyth	8.2	London	6.2
Blackpool	8.7	Margate	5.8
Bournemouth	10.7	Morecambe	10.9
Brighton	4.5	Newquay	3.8
Eastbourne	5.0	Penzance	2.1
Glasgow	2.2	Sandown	9.6
Gt. Yarmouth	13.4		

How many hours of sunshine did London have yesterday?

Name the sunniest place (or places) yesterday.

Which town had the least sunshine?

How many towns had more than twelve hours of sunshine?

How many towns had less than six hours of sunshine?

Forecasting the Weather

Besides telling us about the weather of the immediate past, the newspaper tells us what it is likely to be in the immediate future. The latter is what is known as a *weather forecast*.

Usually the country is divided up into districts, and a separate forecast is given for each district. The forecast includes the expected highest (*maximum*) temperature for the period in that district. Here is an example of a forecast for 6 a.m. to midnight for London and south-east England:

> Some rain, brighter later. Wind S., moderate or fresh. Westerly later. Max. 13° C., 55° F.

Is any rain expected today? If so, early or late?

Will the weather get worse or better during the day?

From what direction is the wind likely to blow at first?

How is the wind going to change?

What will be the highest temperature?

Along with the day's forecast is a brief *outlook* for the next two days.

> *Outlook*: Showers everywhere. Some sunny intervals.

The Weather Chart

Some newspapers print a weather map, or weather chart, of Europe and the North Atlantic Ocean. It is a forecast chart of what the weather is expected to be at noon over that area. Look closely at the chart below.

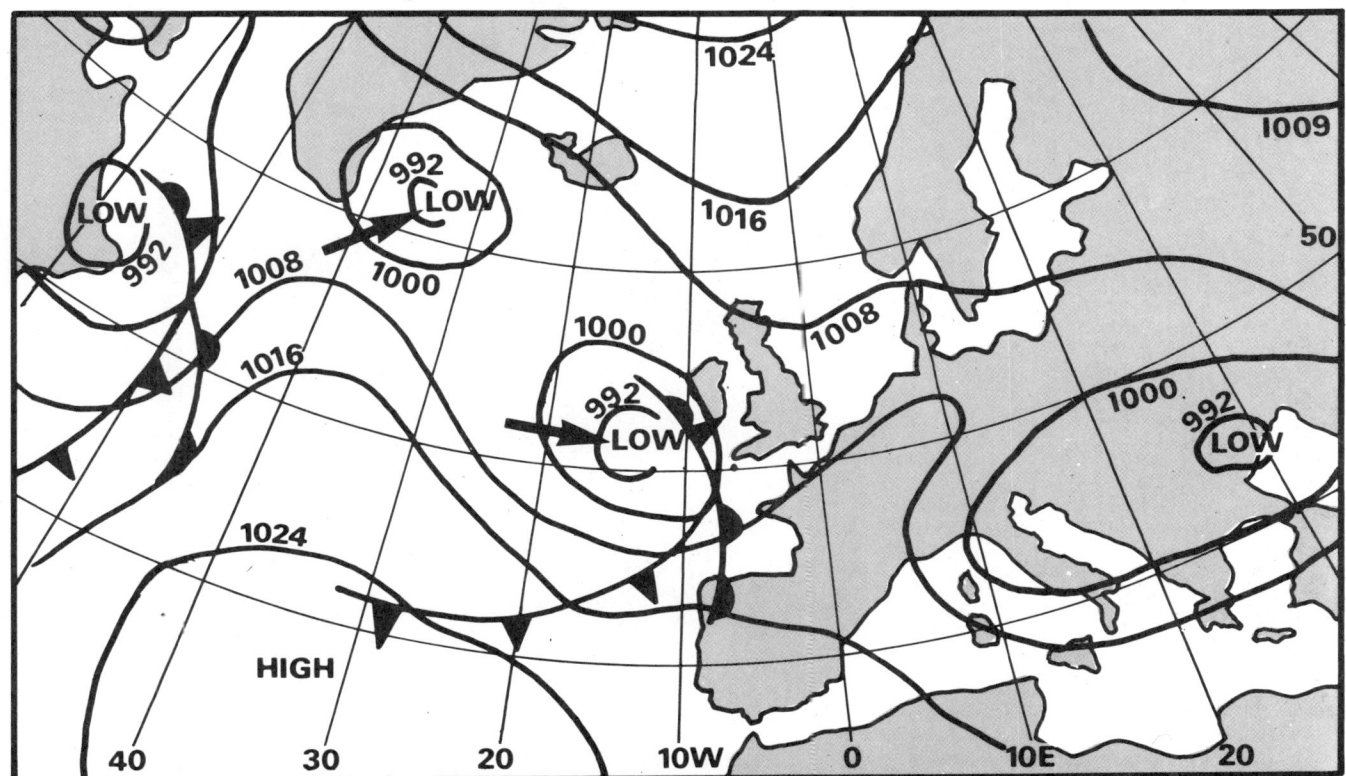

The curved lines on the chart are *isobars*—lines joining places with equal *atmospheric pressure*: the figures on these lines say what the atmospheric pressure is in *millibars*.

Areas where the pressure is lowest are marked LOW. They are called *depressions*, and are areas of unsettled weather. Areas of high pressure are marked HIGH; these are *anticyclones*, and within them the weather is generally calm and settled.

The thick lines with symbols along them are *fronts*; the symbols are placed on the side towards which the front is moving. These fronts show where one kind of air changes to another. The *warm front*, for instance, shows where cool air (ahead) changes to warm air (behind). It is drawn thus: ●●●●●

The *cold front*, showing where warm air changes to cool or cold air, is drawn thus: ▲▲▲▲

As these fronts travel along, the cold front begins to overtake the warm front where they are close together, and converts it into an *occluded front*, or *occlusion*, which is drawn thus: ●▲●▲▲

How many depressions are there on the above chart?
How many occluded fronts are there?
What is the lowest indicated pressure on the chart?
What is the highest pressure?
Look at the depression just west of the British Isles: what are the latitude and longitude (approximately) of its centre?
Which do you think has the more settled weather, S.W. Ireland or S.W. Spain?

The weather in the previous picture (p. 72) would be described by the letter 's' (sunny), but for the weather in this picture the letter 'r' (rain) would certainly be used: here we see heavy monsoon rain falling in India.

You might like to find out more about the weather, weather charts, and weather forecasting, and even try your hand as a forecaster. If so, you will find these small books helpful:

The Observer's Book of Weather (Warne), by R. M. Lester, The Amateur Weather Forecaster (Harrap), by Ernest S. Gates.

TIMETABLES

Up till the nineteenth century people had to live within walking distance of their work.

The coming of cheap transport changed all that. People could travel in to work from out-of-town and travel home again in the evening.

The first railway in the world was opened in Britain in 1825. By 1865 most of the country had been covered by a network of railway lines and cheap workmen's trains were running to and from the cities at a charge of only a penny for twelve miles.

Another development was the omnibus. At first these buses were pulled by horses and had open tops. The first one appeared in London's streets in 1828. It wasn't till just before the First World War that this type of bus was finally driven off the roads by the new motorized buses.

Find the origin of the word *omnibus* in your dictionary.

As public transport became more and more common, *timetables* became essential.

Here is a simple bus timetable.

OUTWARD   **N Su**

Parness (Station)	5.20 a.m.	5.39 a.m.	Every	10.39 p.m.	11.09 p.m.
Trierly (West Cross)	5.28 a.m.	5.47 a.m.	30 minutes	10.47 p.m.	11.17 p.m.
Shieldhill (Alexander St)	5.31 a.m.	5.50 a.m.	thereafter	10.50 p.m.	11.20 p.m.
Milltown (Town Hall)	5.44 a.m.	6.03 a.m.	until	11.03 p.m.	11.33 p.m.
Milltown (Nether Road)	5.47 a.m.	6.06 a.m.		11.06 p.m.	11.36 p.m.

INWARD   **N Su**

Milltown (Nether Road)	5.47 a.m.	6.06 a.m.	Every	11.06 p.m.	11.36 p.m.
Milltown (Town Hall)	5.53 a.m.	6.12 a.m.	30 minutes	11.12 p.m.	11.42 p.m.
Shieldhill (Alexander St)	6.06 a.m.	6.25 a.m.	thereafter	11.25 p.m.	11.55 p.m.
Trierly (West Cross)	6.09 a.m.	6.28 a.m.	until	11.28 p.m.	11.58 p.m.
Parness (Station)	6.17 a.m.	6.36 a.m.		11.36 a.m.	

N Su = Except Sunday

If you wish to reach Milltown Town Hall by 6 a.m. what bus must you take from Parness?

How long does it take to travel by bus from Trierly to Milltown (Nether Road)?

You live in Parness and go to school in Shieldhill. At what time must you leave in the morning to get to school for 9 o'clock?

At what time would you get back to Parness if school closes at 4 o'clock?

You live in Shieldhill but go to a Saturday night party in Milltown. If you travel home on the last bus, at what time do you arrive in Shieldhill?

You travel from Parness to Milltown every Sunday to see your grandmother. What is the last possible bus you can take home?

The Twenty-Four-Hour Clock

Many timetables use the 24-hour clock.

> 1 a.m.   is 01.00
>
> 6 a.m.   is 06.00
>
> Mid-day is 12.00

After that you imagine the clock going round for the second time.

> 1 p.m. becomes 13.00
>
> 3 p.m. becomes 15.00
>
> 4.30 p.m. becomes 16.30
>
> 10.15 p.m. becomes 22.15
>
> Midnight becomes 24.00

Turn these into 12-hour clock times (remember a.m. or p.m.):

07.15   13.30   16.10   17.45   22.00   23.59

Turn these into 24-hour clock times:

6.15 a.m.   1.40 p.m.   3.36 p.m.   7.20 p.m.
10.30 p.m.   11.45 p.m.

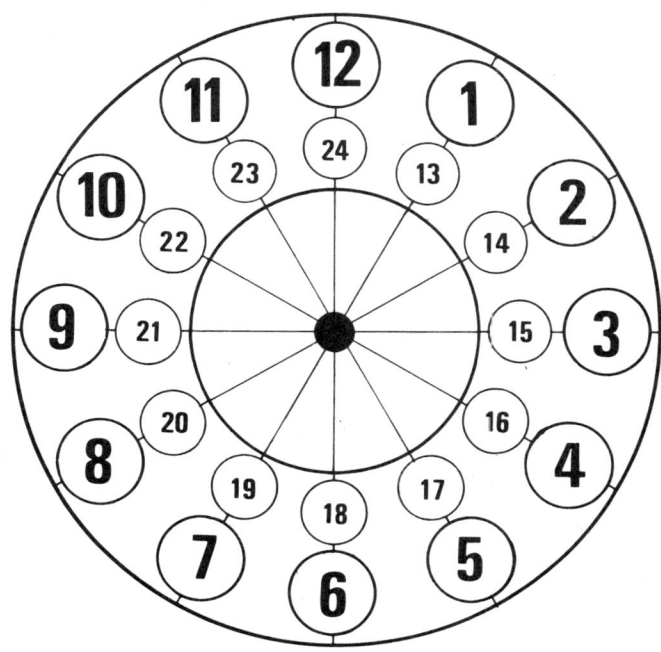

A workmen's train arriving at Victoria Station, London, 1865.

Here is a railway timetable using the twenty-four hour clock.

OUTWARD	N Su				N Su				S Su
Polville		0819	1035		1235	1435	1635	1835	2235
Marywell		0844	1100	1210	1300	1500	1700	1900	2300
Hilledge		0920	1136	1246	1336	1536	1736	1936	2336
Heathway		0930	1146	1256	1346	1546	1746	1946	2346
Lilyhead		0942	1158	1308	1358	1553	1758	1958	2358
Marchbank	0759	0953	1209	1319	1409	1609	1809	2009	0009
St Glespard	0802	0956	1212						
Woodvale	0805	0959	1215						
Besterton	0845	1040	1255						

INWARD	N Su				N Su				S Su
Besterton			0854		1254		1654		2054
Woodvale			0934	1134	1334		1734		2134
St Glespard			0937	1137	1337		1737		2147
Marchbank	0636	0736	0940	1140	1340	1540	1740	1940	2150
Lilyhead	0647	0747	0951	1151	1351	1551	1751	1951	2202
Heathway	0659	0759	1003	1203	1403	1603	1803	2003	
Hilledge	0709	0809	1013	1213	1413	1613	1813	2013	
Marywell	0745	0845	1050	1250	1450	1650	1850	2050	
Polville	0810	0910	1116	1315	1515	1715	1915	2115	

S Su = Saturday & Sunday only   **N Su = Except Sunday**

You live in Lilyhead and travel by the first train on Monday to Besterton. At what time do you arrive?

A woman sets out to catch the 1210 train from Marywell, but misses it. What is the earliest she can now arrive in Marchbank?

You visit a friend in Lilyhead on Friday evening and come home on the last train to Polville. At what time do you arrive?

Your uncle is staying with you for the weekend at Polville. He doesn't leave till the last train on Sunday night. At what time does he get home to Marchbank?

What is the earliest that a man from St Glespard can be in Besterton on Sunday morning if he travels by train?

Many people nowadays travel by plane. Here is a typical airport destination board.

Aircraft Type	DC8	747	DC10	747	VC	747	707	747	707
Flight Number	IB 966	TP 250	SA 281	SA 234	BA 052	BA 032	SN 328	SA 222	SA 266
Class of Travel	F/Y	F/Y	F/Y	F/Y	F/Y	F/Y	F/Y	F/Y	F/Y
ROME								1050	
ATHENS									0845
ZURICH			0600						
FRANKFURT				0815					
BRUSSELS							0640		
LONDON					0600	0610			

Footnotes
Class of Travel   **F = First Class**   **Y = Economy Class**

Airlines and Aircraft Type
BA = British Airways   **= VC10/Boeing 747**
IB = Iberia   **= DC8**
SA = South African Airways = Boeing 707/747
SN = Sabena   **= Boeing 707**
TP = Portuguese Airways = Boeing 707/747

By which airline would you be flown to the following places?

Brussels   Rome   Zurich

When the loudspeaker at an airport announces the departure of planes it uses their flight numbers.

What is the destination of each of the following flights? **SA 234   SN 328   BA 052**

At what time does the first plane in the morning leave for London?

What is its flight number?

To which airline does it belong?

On which type of plane would you fly to Athens?

Could you book a first class seat on it?

FINDING YOUR WAY ABOUT A CITY

If you wish to find your way about a strange city you need the help of a guide book or a special kind of map called a street map.

Below is part of a street map of central London showing many of the areas much visited by tourists.

Find out all you can about the following landmarks from an encyclopaedia, guide book or any other reference book:

Westminster Abbey   Lambeth Palace
The Cenotaph

Find the following places on your street map:

Constitution Hill   Westminster Bridge
Whitehall   Strand

Look at the map and decide how you would go from Marble Arch to Fleet Street.

Name three London parks.

Give the names of all the bridges over the Thames that are shown in this map.

Which route would you take from Hyde Park Corner to Euston Station?

1. *Buckingham Palace, The Mall.*

3. *Horse Guards Parade, Whitehall.*

2. *Houses of Parliament by Westminster Bridge.*

4. *Trafalgar Square with St Martin's in the Fields*

Here are photographs of four famous London landmarks. Can you find the places on your street map?

The Underground

One of the most convenient ways of travelling about London is by the Underground. The Underground stations are marked on our map by this symbol ⊖ Find some of them on the map.

Here is a map of the complete London Underground.
As you can see, it consists of several different lines.
Some stations, however, are at the junction of more
than one line. These are the stations where you can
change to another line.

To get from *Finchley Road* in the north, for instance, to
Stockwell in the south, you travel on the *Bakerloo* line
to *Elephant & Castle* where you change to the *Northern*
line.

How do you get from Victoria to each of the following
stations?

Baker Street   **Upminster**
Paddington   **Ealing Broadway**

Designed by Paul E. Garbutt
Copyright London Transport Executive

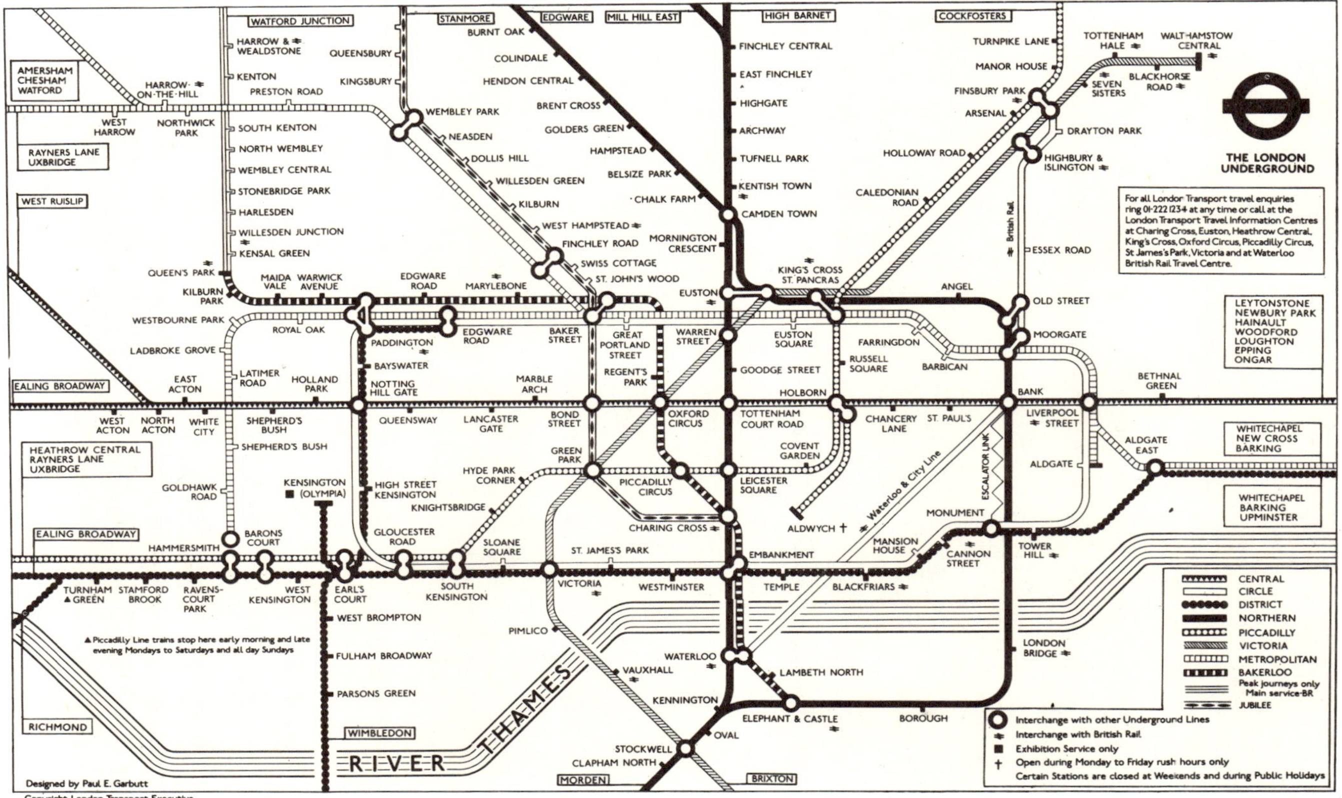

a shelf of books

Look at the books shown here. Which would you use to look up the following information?

The meaning of a Spanish word.
Birds of South America.
The jackal and where it lives.
The dates of Jane Austen.
Growing dahlias.
Space satellites.
The works of Beethoven.

The life of the actor David Garrick.
Who said, 'What I tell you three times is true'?
A Gresley Pacific locomotive.
The life of Leonardo da Vinci.
How many sons had Priam, king of Troy?
What is the name of the Duke of Illyria in
Twelfth-Night by William Shakespeare?
A particular issue of postage stamp.

Now give names of other reference books you would need to look up the following:

The population of a country.
The phone number of a friend.
The name of a good hotel in a town you intend to visit.
The school which a famous politician attended.
Which of two towns is further east.
The fourth Commandment.
The licensing hours in a market town.
The capital of a little-known country.
The Christian name (or initials) of your doctor.
Which parts of an area are mountainous and which parts are flat.
The name of a fungus.
How many children a famous living author has.
The whereabouts of the main London stations.
The largest bulldozer in the world.
Whether you are likely to have rain today.
The story of the first Christmas.
The inventor of the "spinning jenny".
For what is Edward Jenner famous?
When was the battle of Agincourt?
Who was Rasputin?
When is early closing day in Shrewsbury?

Here are the names of the people who invented or discovered the six objects on this page:

G. Marconi   **Sir Frank Whittle**
Sir Humphrey Davy   **Sir Alexander Fleming**
Galileo   **John Logie Baird**

Using any reference book you like, link the correct name with each invention.

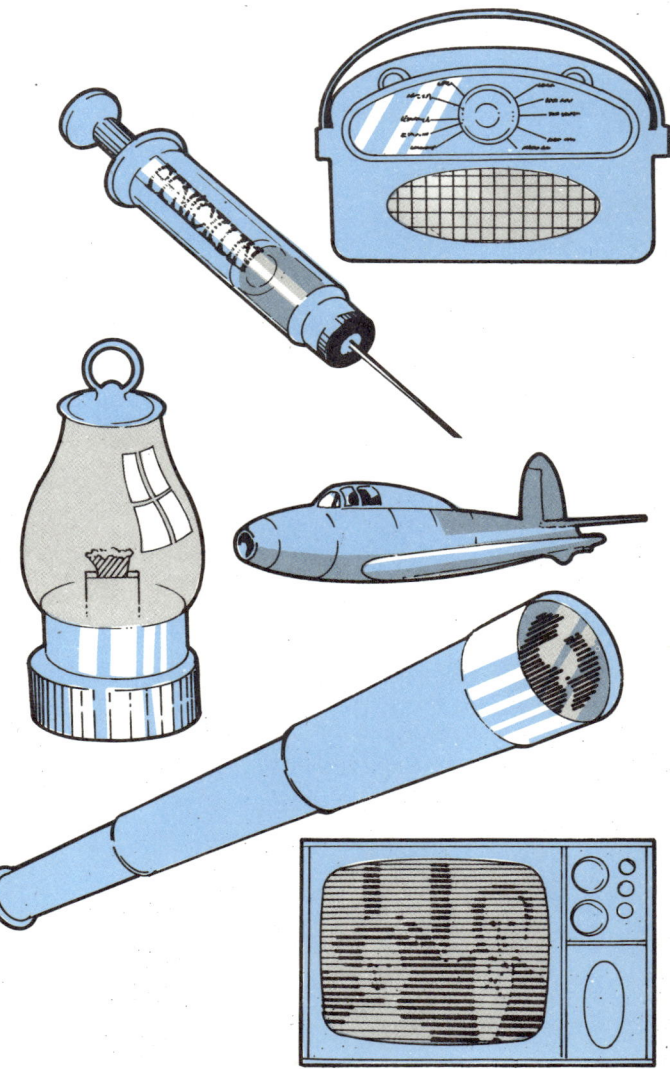

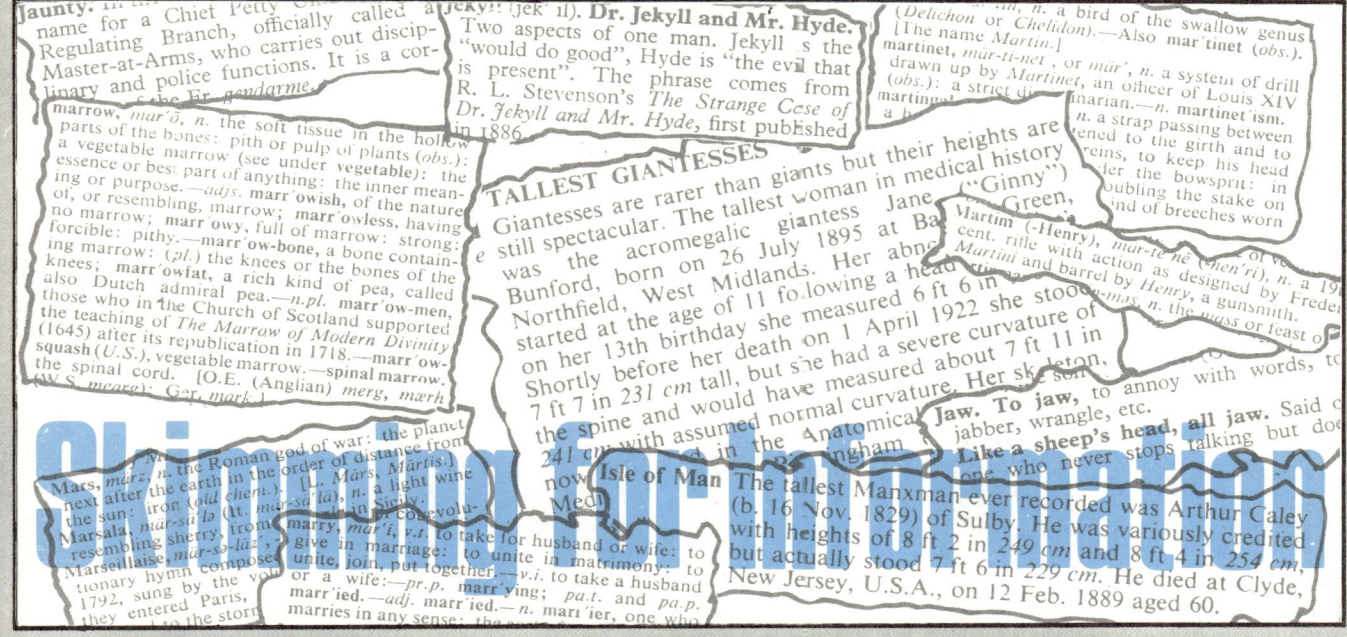

One of the skills needed when working with reference books is the knack of *skimming for information*. That means you *hurry through all the information given*, skimming over it *until you come to the detail you want*. Look at this page from a reference book, shown opposite.

Find the answers to these questions by skimming quickly through the information given until you come to the fact you are seeking.

Three of these men were alive at the same time. Can you name them?

    Which two were writers?

    Which two were Americans?

    Which one lived longest?

    Who was a king?

    Which one wrote a book while in prison?

    Who was hanged?

What two jobs did William Cody have during his lifetime?

Who died when he was sixty years old?

If you wanted someone to teach you Italian, which one would you choose?

What was King Robert I's dying wish?

Who had a song written about him?

Whose wife was called Elizabeth?

Which one had the shortest life?

BROWN, John. An American born in 1800. He wanted to abolish slavery and led a raid on the arsenal at Harper's Ferry to seize the guns. He was hanged for treason in 1859, but is remembered in the song "John Brown's Body Lies A-Mouldering In The Grave, But His Soul Goes Marching On".

BROWNING, Robert. English poet, born in London in 1812. In 1846 he married Elizabeth Barrett, another poet, and went to live in Italy. His best known poem is probably "The Pied Piper of Hamelin". He died in England in 1889.

BRUCE, Robert. Became King Robert I of Scotland. In 1314, at the age of 40, he defeated Edward II of England at the battle of Bannockburn and gained Scotland its independence. After his death in 1329 his heart was taken on a crusade in accordance with his dying request.

BUFFALO BILL. Born in America in 1845 as William Cody, he gained his nickname when he became the hunter responsible for providing buffalo meat for the workmen building the Pacific Railway. Later he became a showman with a travelling Wild West show and died in 1917.

BUNYAN, John. English author, born in Bedfordshire in 1628. In his busy life he held many jobs—tinker, soldier, preacher. His masterpiece is "Pilgrim's Progress" which was written in prison. He died in 1688.

Skimming For Information In Your Encyclopaedia

Find the date of birth of the following:

William Shakespeare

Oliver Cromwell

Sir Walter Raleigh

Ferdinand Magellan

Johann Sebastian Bach

In Your Gazetteer

In which country is each of these towns?

Zagreb   Cologne   Valparaiso

Shanghai   Durban

Practice in Speedy Skimming

Find any subject in an encyclopaedia, preferably one that takes up about half a page. You are going to pick out quickly four facts that you think are important and then write them down. Read fast and try to train your mind to skip over all the other details that you don't need.

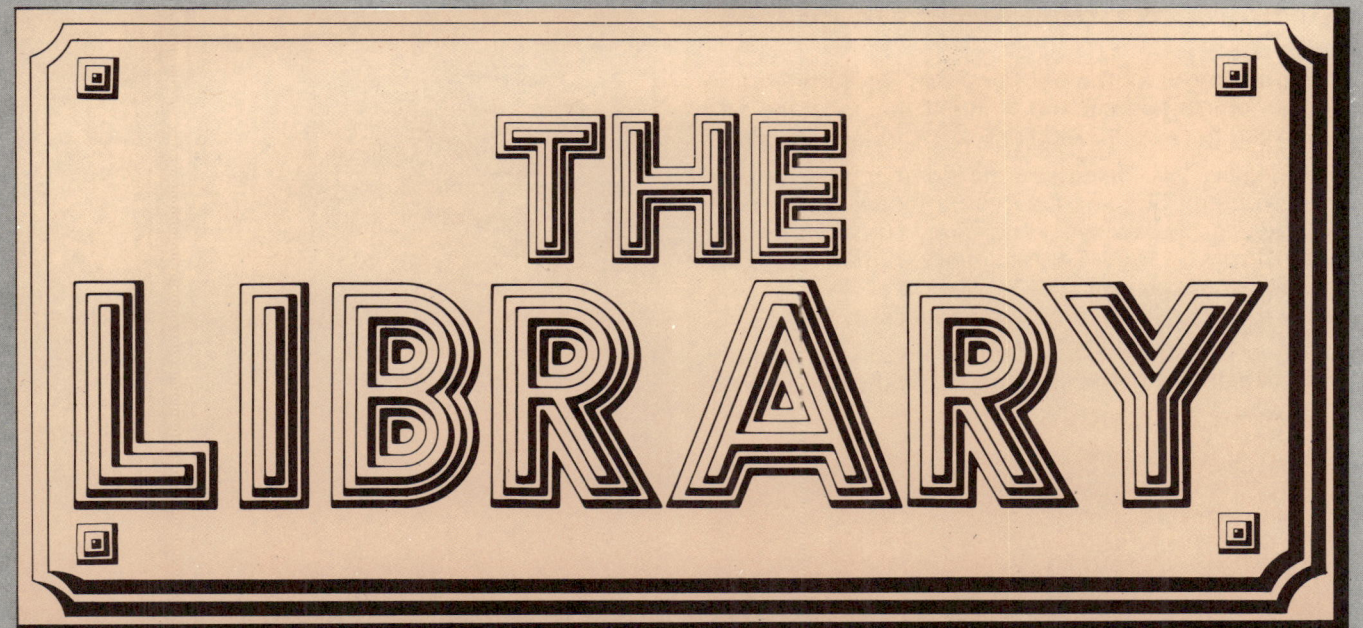

THE LIBRARY

As you have gone through this book you have concentrated on reference works, like encyclopaedias, dictionaries and atlases. These make useful starting points and the information in them is usually well set out and easy to find.

When you go to the public library you will find a Reference Section there too. But these books may only be used in the library, so you must take a notebook with you to jot down the information you find. There are also hundreds of other books which you *are* allowed to borrow and take away with you. A library is a wonderful mine of information waiting to be used. But how do you begin to dig it out?

The first thing to remember is that all the books in a library are carefully classified—arranged according to their subjects. You must get to know the subject headings: Biography, History, Languages, Literature, Travel, Useful Arts, for instance. The best way is to ask the librarian to help you. She will show you exactly where to look for the subject you want.

If there is a Children's Section you will soon find your way around it. In the picture on this page the boys and girls with their backs to the camera are in the Children's Library looking at books on transport. Where the encyclopaedia can give you a general idea about transport, special books can go into far more detail. If you are keen to know about cars, railways, monorails or supersonic flight there will be books to suit you. This type of book is known as 'non-fiction' because it deals with real facts, while a 'fiction' book is imaginative writing—perhaps a story, poetry or plays.

Getting Extra Help from the Request Service

If you have got all the help you can from the library, both in the Reference and General Sections and still haven't found exactly what you want, what do you do?

Once again, you go to see the librarian and explain your problem. She will give you a request card to fill in. Then the library will send away for more books, usually from a bigger central library. When the books you asked for come in, your own library will let you know that they are ready to be collected.

The two boys in the photograph are at the Enquiry Desk explaining to the librarian about the extra books they would like.

Make a Guide to Your Library

Imagine that a new boy or girl has come to your school and wants to know about the local library.

Make a little guide to the library. Show where it is by drawing a map. Write down the opening times. Describe what you have to do to join. Draw a plan of the inside of the library and show where the various subjects are kept. Show where the Reference Section is and also the Children's Library.

FACTS AND TOPI AND TOPIC WOR TOPIC WORK FAC WORK FACTS AN

Finding facts is not always enough. When you undertake a project on a subject you are being asked first to get hold of the information and then to arrange it. So planning is important.

In the next few pages you will see some outlines for projects. They show you how, from one main theme, you can start thinking in many different directions. You will notice, too, how all your school subjects, from maths to English, have some bearing on the theme.

One thing is clear, though. If you intend to produce a really good project you have some fascinating discoveries ahead of you, and the more books you can look up, the better the result will be.

Plan Your Fact-Seeking

Try making a typical work-scheme for a project. Suppose you want to do CANADA.

Make a rough plan of how you would set about collecting your information. It might be something like this:

PROJECT: CANADA

Go to school or class library →

Start with encyclopaedias, atlases.
Look for books on history and geography of Canada; life in Canada, famous Canadians.

See the librarian and explain what you need. Ask for her advice. Try the Reference Section.
Find the subject section and choose the books that will be most useful. Make a note of other titles to borrow later when you bring back the first books.

Go to public library →

Look around at home and elsewhere →

Try to find pictures, cuttings from newspapers and magazines, postcards, stamps, travel brochures of Canada.

You will find a project outline for Canada on pages 92-93.

English
Dictionary Work

bow	galleon	ballast
stern	coracle	bilge
rudder	dug-out	bulwark
forecastle	canoe	bulkhead
poop	hovercraft	companionway
porthole	galley	davits
keel	clipper	hatchway
hull	steamer	knot
hold	schooner	nautical
port	raft	mile
starboard	longship	

Maths

Plotting courses
Measuring distances
Bearings
Mariner's compass
Scale drawings
Scale models

Music

Sea Shanties

Pirates

Canals

SHI

English
Literature

Prose

Treasure Island	: Stevenson
Moby Dick	: Melville
Coral Island	: Ballantyne
Robinson Crusoe	: Defoe

Poetry

Sea Fever	: Masefield
Three Fishers	: Kingsley
Drake's Drum	: Masefield
Christmas At Sea	: Stevenson
Cargoes	: Masefield
Flannan Isle	: Gibson
Last Buccaneer	: Kingsley
Ancient Mariner	: Coleridge
Down On The Shore	: Allingham
The Inchcape Rock	: Southey

Abbreviations

H.M.S.
S.S.
S.Y.
R.M.S.
M.N.
R.N.
R.A.N.
R.C.N.
U.S.N.
U.S.S.

History & Geography

Biographical Dictionary
& Encyclopaedia Work

Vasco da Gama
Ferdinand Magellan
Captain Cook
Christopher Columbus
Sir Francis Drake
Abel Tasman

Plot voyages of above

PS

History of Shipping Biographical Dictionary & Encyclopaedia Work
Henry Bell
Samuel Plimsoll
William Symington
Robert Fulton
Samuel Cunard
I. K. Brunel
C. S. Cockerell
Samuel Morse

Bible
Noah's Ark
Journeys of Paul
Fishing on the
Sea of Galilee
Jonah

Arts & Crafts
Paintings
Models
Silhouettes
Collages
of famous ships
   e.g.
Santa Maria
Mayflower
Golden Hind
Comet
HMS Victory
Savannah
Great Western
Marie Celeste
HMS Bounty
Titanic
Queen Mary
Queen Elizabeth
Q.E.II

Docks & Harbours

Fishing

Science
Floating
Sinking
Displacement
Plimsoll Line
Winds
Meteorology
Stars
Tides
Steam
Hovercraft
   principle

Reference Work & Illustrating

Merchant Ships		**Warships**
tug	lifeboat	submarine
drifter	cableship	destroyer
trawler	lightship	aircraft carrier
oil tanker	container ship	landing craft
whaler	dredger	minesweeper
whale factory	ice breaker	minelayer
ship	ferry	battleship
		cruiser

History
Encyclopaedia or
Biographical Dictionary
Work:
John Cabot
Sebastian Cabot
Jacques Cartier
Samuel Champlain
Governor Du Quesne
Martin Frobisher
Sir Humphrey Gilbert
Henry Hudson
William Mackenzie
General Montcalm
General Wolfe

Collections
Stamps
Coins
Labels
Postcards
Photographs
Magazine and
newspaper clippings

Royal Canadian
Mounted Police

CAN

Dictionary Work
moccasin
wampum
totem
calumet
squaw
papoose
reservation
wigwam
tomahawk

Red Indians
Apache
Iroquois
Algonquin
Sioux
Blackfoot
Mohawks
Dakotas

Arts & Crafts
Painting of
Canadian flag
Model Indian
encampment
Large model
totem poles
Eskimo doll
Red Indian doll
R.C.M.P. doll
Lumberjack doll

Music
Canadian National
Anthem
French-Canadian
songs, e.g. Alouette, etc.

Geography
Mapwork
Distance by
air to rest
of the world
Tourist agency
material
Sea routes

Products
Wheat
Furs
Apples
Salmon
Cod
Paper (wood
pulp)

Reference Work
Gazetteer
Ottawa
Winnipeg
Montreal
Toronto
Vancouver
Quebec
Great Lakes
Rocky Mountains
St Lawrence
Hudson Bay

ADA

Eskimos

Mathematics
Population graphs (or
bargraphs) of
Canadian provinces
Piechart showing
percentage of
French Canadians
in population of
Canada
Graphs comparing
population of
Canada with
population of other
countries
Time zones in
Canada
Canadian dollars and
foreign exchange
equivalents

Sport
Ice hockey
Canada's
record in
Olympic and
Commonwealth
Games

Literature
Books by
J. Fenimore
Cooper
Oxford Book
of Canadian
Verse.

Mathematics

Seconds, minutes, hours, days, weeks, months, years, etc.

Timetables

Calendar work

The 24-hour clock

Science

Movement of the Sun and Stars

Experiments with stick stuck in ground and with shadows

What exactly is
a day?   a month?   a year?

Why do we get
summer?   winter?

English
Origins

Find the origins of the names of the days of the week (i.e. Sunday, Monday, etc.) and the names of the months (i.e. January, February, etc.)

English
Dictionary Work

decade

century

millenium

& other words denoting time

Bible
The Creation

Arts & Crafts
Paint pictures of the four seasons
Make a "permanent" calendar

History of Timekeeping
Encyclopaedia Work
Sundial
Water-clock
Sand-clock
Candle-clock
Pendulum

Biographical Dictionary Work
Peter Henlein
Galileo
Christian Huyghens

Creative Writing

Write a story about being ship-wrecked on a desert island and how you keep track of time

Write a story entitled "The Time Machine"

Geography

Seasons in different parts of the world

Time differences in different parts of the world

The International Dateline

Reference Work

Find the dates of the following and all the information you can about each one:

Christmas Day

Boxing Day

St David's Day

St George's Day

St Patrick's Day

St Valentine's Day

St Andrew's Day

The Shortest Day

The Longest Day

Armistice Day (World War I)

D-Day (World War II)

Hallowe'en

April Fools Day

Independence Day (U.S.A.)

Bastille Day (France)

Guy Fawkes Day

Thanksgiving Day (U.S.A.)

Thanksgiving Day (Canada)

Columbus Day (U.S.A.)

May Day

St Swithin's Day

ME

English Literature

Prose

Any science fiction dealing with the future or with moving from one age to another, e.g. Dr Who

Poetry

Spring	: Nash
The Year	: Patmore
Summer	: Rossetti
To Autumn	: Keats
The Death of the Old Year	: Tennyson
Easter	: Herbert
London Snow	: Bridges

ACKNOWLEDGEMENTS

Our thanks are due to the Parkway Group for the design, lay-out and typography.

We are grateful to W. G. Moore, B.Sc., F.R.G.S. who contributed the chapter 'Daily News Daily Weather' and also to the following for kindly allowing us to reproduce copyright material and photographs in this book:

A. & C. Black Ltd., Publishers: extract from 'Black's Children's Encyclopaedia'; Hamish Hamilton Children's Books Ltd.: extract from 'A Children's Working Dictionary' by Arthur J. Arkley; Penguin Books Ltd.: extract from 'A Dictionary of Chivalry' (Longman 1968) by Grant Uden; Associated Book Publishers Ltd.: extracts from 'When We Were Very Young' and 'Now We are Six' by A. A. Milne; Pelham Books Ltd.: extract from 'Pears Cyclopaedia'; Guinness Superlatives Ltd.: extracts from 'The Guinness Book of Records'; The Bodley Head: extract from 'Going Down Hill on a Bicycle' by Henry Beeching; Oxford University Press: 'The Oxford Dictionary of Quotations'.

Photographs: The cover photograph and the illustrations showing children using a library were taken in Chesham Library, by kind permission of R. C. Howes, County Reference Librarian, Buckinghamshire, and Miss Pepper, Librarian, Chesham Library who generously made their facilities available. The photography is by Robert Glover Studio, Amersham.

Other photographs appearing in the book were supplied by:

Central Office of Information Photographs Library; Trust Houses Forte Ltd.; The Photographic Library of the Australian Information Service; The Rev. J. C. Allen; The Encyclopaedia Britannica; Radio Times Hulton Library; Will Green; Ordnance Survey Ltd.: Map of Visitor's London; The Hamlyn Group: covers of 'The Giant All-Colour Dictionary' and Larousse Encyclopaedias; Macmillan, London and Basingstoke: cover design and pp. 92 and 93 of 'Macmillan's Our World Encyclopaedia' Volume 1; London Transport Board: map of London Underground and photographs of London; W. & R. Chambers Ltd.: cover of 'Chambers Twentieth Century Dictionary'; J. Allan Cash, Ltd.; M. J. R. Smith; K.L.M. Airlines; Sun Photographic Bureau, Amersham.

Our thanks are also due to G. E. Kerridge, of Kerridge's, Amersham for his kind cooperation in allowing photographs to be taken in the book department.

ISBN 0 7175 0751 3

First published 1977
by Hulton Educational Publications Ltd.,
Raans Road, Amersham, Bucks.

Printed in Great Britain by Martin's of Berwick